Maths Activity Workbook

For Kids Ages 4-6

This Book Belongs to

_____

Copyright © 2024

All rights reserved. No part of this publication may be reproduced, distributed, or transmitted in any form or by any means, including photocopying, recording, or other electronic or mechanical methods, without the prior written permission of the publisher.

Comibine your number writing skills and practice the numbers below

Addition

Answer the following Addition based questions.

1) 8 + 7 =
2) 3 + 6 =
3) 8 + 8 =
4) 1 + 2 =
5) 6 + 4 =
6) 3 + 1 =
7) 4 + 9 =
8) 8 + 1 =
9) 3 + 1 =
10) 9 + 1 =
11) 4 + 8 =
12) 9 + 4 =

Addition

Answer the following Addition based questions.

1) 9 + 7 = ☐   2) 8 + 5 = ☐

3) 4 + 1 = ☐   4) 9 + 4 = ☐

5) 3 + 2 = ☐   6) 3 + 1 = ☐

7) 5 + 3 = ☐   8) 8 + 4 = ☐

9) 6 + 1 = ☐   10) 7 + 4 = ☐

11) 8 + 9 = ☐   12) 5 + 9 = ☐

Addition

Answer the following Addition based questions.

1) 3 + 3 = ☐   2) 1 + 1 = ☐

3) 2 + 1 = ☐   4) 9 + 7 = ☐

5) 4 + 8 = ☐   6) 9 + 4 = ☐

7) 5 + 9 = ☐   8) 4 + 9 = ☐

9) 5 + 1 = ☐   10) 7 + 3 = ☐

11) 4 + 3 = ☐   12) 4 + 8 = ☐

Addition

Fill in the gap to make the Addition question complete.

1) $7 + \square = 16$ 2) $5 + \square = 9$

3) $9 + \square = 17$ 4) $1 + \square = 6$

5) $6 + \square = 8$ 6) $3 + \square = 7$

7) $3 + \square = 4$ 8) $8 + \square = 17$

9) $4 + \square = 7$ 10) $5 + \square = 7$

11) $1 + \square = 10$ 12) $5 + \square = 11$

Addition

Fill in the gap to make the Addition question complete.

1) $4 + \boxed{} = 10$ 2) $5 + \boxed{} = 12$

3) $7 + \boxed{} = 9$ 4) $1 + \boxed{} = 5$

5) $2 + \boxed{} = 7$ 6) $1 + \boxed{} = 8$

7) $8 + \boxed{} = 10$ 8) $5 + \boxed{} = 7$

9) $5 + \boxed{} = 14$ 10) $7 + \boxed{} = 8$

11) $7 + \boxed{} = 9$ 12) $8 + \boxed{} = 11$

Addition

Fill in the gap to make the Addition question complete.

1) $7 + \boxed{} = 8$ 2) $4 + \boxed{} = 5$

3) $7 + \boxed{} = 13$ 4) $7 + \boxed{} = 14$

5) $3 + \boxed{} = 4$ 6) $4 + \boxed{} = 13$

7) $7 + \boxed{} = 16$ 8) $1 + \boxed{} = 10$

9) $2 + \boxed{} = 10$ 10) $8 + \boxed{} = 14$

11) $6 + \boxed{} = 15$ 12) $6 + \boxed{} = 12$

Addition

Answer the following Addition based questions.

1)
```
    8
+ 2 0
-----
```

2)
```
  1 7
+ 1 1
-----
```

3)
```
  1 1
+   2
-----
```

4)
```
    3
+ 1 2
-----
```

5)
```
    7
+ 1 5
-----
```

6)
```
    3
+ 1 1
-----
```

7)
```
  1 6
+ 1 2
-----
```

8)
```
    9
+ 1 1
-----
```

9)
```
  1 4
+ 2 0
-----
```

10)
```
  1 4
+ 1 2
-----
```

11)
```
  1 8
+   6
-----
```

12)
```
    7
+ 1 3
-----
```

Addition

Answer the following Addition based questions.

1)   2 + 13

2)   12 + 9

3)   14 + 9

4)   13 + 19

5)   16 + 7

6)   15 + 19

7)   3 + 19

8)   9 + 17

9)   5 + 18

10)   13 + 12

11)   19 + 2

12)   18 + 19

Addition

Answer the following Addition based questions.

1)   12
   + 1

2)   17
   + 10

3)   3
   + 8

4)   10
   + 8

5)   17
   + 17

6)   17
   + 4

7)   15
   + 5

8)   16
   + 18

9)   4
   + 8

10) 19
   + 4

11) 18
   + 16

12) 10
   + 4

Addition

Answer the following Addition based questions.

1) 17
  + 17

2)   8
  + 7

3) 19
  + 5

4) 16
  + 17

5)   6
  + 2

6)   2
  + 8

7) 19
  + 5

8) 18
  + 3

9) 16
  + 5

10) 19
  + 18

11) 5
  + 13

12) 10
  + 15

Addition

Count the number of pictures and add together.

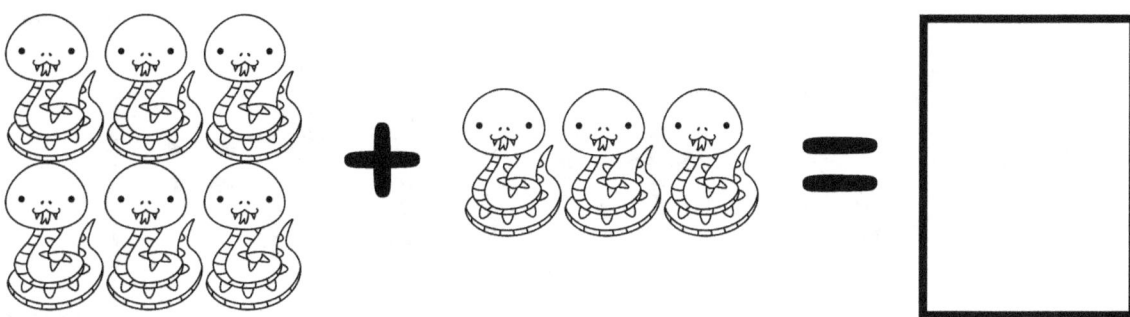

_____   _____

_____   _____

_____   _____

Addition

Count the number of pictures and add together.

_____   _____

_____   _____

_____   _____

Addition

Work out the answer to the following Addition based questions.

4 + 🍓🍓🍓 = ☐

15 + 🐉🐉🐉🐉 = ☐

12 + 🦊🦊🦊🦊🦊 = ☐

Addition

Work out the answer to the following Addition based questions.

4 + 🏐🏐🏐🏐🏐🏐 = ☐

___

15 + ☂☂☂ = ☐

___

12 + 🐯 = ☐

___

Addition

Work out the answer to the following Addition based questions.

🛸🛸🛸 + 11 = ☐

___

🚂🚂🚂🚂🚂🚂 + 9 = ☐

___

🐍🐍🐍🐍 + 14 = ☐

___

Addition

Work out the answer to the following Addition based questions.

🐚🐚🐚 + 10 = ☐

___

🦈 + 7 = ☐

___

👑👑 + 3 = ☐

___

Addition

Work out the answer to the following Addition based questions.

There are some robots playing in the park. 3 robots are playing on the swings, 2 robots are playing on the slide. How many robots are playing in the park in total?

_____

There are 8 rabbits hopping in the garden. Then, 3 more rabbits join them. How many rabbits are there in total?

_____

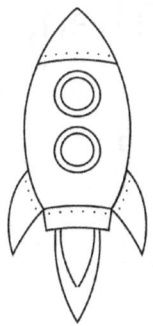
There are 5 spaceships on Planet A. 8 more spaceships land on Planet A. How many spaceships are on Planet A now?

_____

Addition

Work out the answer to the following Addition based questions.

An octopus has 4 fish in one arm and 5 fish in another arm. How many fish does the octopus have in total?

_____

There are 8 mice in the kitchen. 7 more mice come to join them. How many mice are there now?

_____

There are 7 green monsters in the forest. Then, 5 blue monsters join them. How many monsters are there in total?

_____

Subtraction

Answer the following Subtraction based questions.

1) 8 − 3 = ☐
2) 6 − 4 = ☐
3) 4 − 2 = ☐
4) 7 − 6 = ☐
5) 9 − 3 = ☐
6) 8 − 5 = ☐
7) 1 − 1 = ☐
8) 9 − 6 = ☐
9) 7 − 3 = ☐
10) 4 − 1 = ☐
11) 7 − 2 = ☐
12) 5 − 3 = ☐

Subtraction

Answer the following Subtraction based questions.

1) 5 − 4 = ☐   2) 7 − 6 = ☐

3) 7 − 1 = ☐   4) 6 − 2 = ☐

5) 2 − 1 = ☐   6) 9 − 2 = ☐

7) 5 − 5 = ☐   8) 7 − 7 = ☐

9) 5 − 2 = ☐   10) 8 − 7 = ☐

11) 9 − 3 = ☐   12) 7 − 3 = ☐

Subtraction

Answer the following Subtraction based questions.

1) 7 - 6 = ☐
2) 9 - 5 = ☐
3) 9 - 1 = ☐
4) 7 - 4 = ☐
5) 6 - 2 = ☐
6) 4 - 2 = ☐
7) 5 - 4 = ☐
8) 8 - 6 = ☐
9) 4 - 3 = ☐
10) 3 - 3 = ☐
11) 8 - 8 = ☐
12) 2 - 1 = ☐

Subtraction

Fill in the gap to make the Subtraction question complete.

1) 8 − ☐ = 2   2) 8 − ☐ = 2

3) 9 − ☐ = 5   4) 4 − ☐ = 1

5) 2 − ☐ = 0   6) 3 − ☐ = 1

7) 7 − ☐ = 3   8) 1 − ☐ = 0

9) 5 − ☐ = 2   10) 4 − ☐ = 3

11) 8 − ☐ = 7   12) 7 − ☐ = 1

Subtraction

Fill in the gap to make the Subtraction question complete.

1) $8 - \square = 3$ 2) $9 - \square = 1$

3) $5 - \square = 1$ 4) $5 - \square = 0$

5) $7 - \square = 1$ 6) $9 - \square = 8$

7) $7 - \square = 6$ 8) $5 - \square = 2$

9) $8 - \square = 5$ 10) $1 - \square = 0$

11) $6 - \square = 2$ 12) $4 - \square = 2$

Subtraction

Fill in the gap to make the Subtraction question complete.

1) $2 - \Box = 1$ 2) $9 - \Box = 6$

3) $9 - \Box = 3$ 4) $4 - \Box = 2$

5) $7 - \Box = 5$ 6) $4 - \Box = 1$

7) $9 - \Box = 2$ 8) $8 - \Box = 2$

9) $2 - \Box = 1$ 10) $9 - \Box = 3$

11) $6 - \Box = 3$ 12) $6 - \Box = 5$

Subtraction

Answer the following Subtraction based questions.

1) 19 − 6 =

2) 16 − 9 =

3) 14 − 8 =

4) 8 − 8 =

5) 17 − 7 =

6) 9 − 6 =

7) 10 − 5 =

8) 17 − 8 =

9) 7 − 5 =

10) 19 − 17 =

11) 6 − 3 =

12) 20 − 16 =

Subtraction

Answer the following Subtraction based questions.

1) 20 − 17 =

2) 18 − 18 =

3) 11 − 1 =

4) 18 − 6 =

5) 16 − 9 =

6) 13 − 13 =

7) 15 − 9 =

8) 2 − 1 =

9) 6 − 2 =

10) 20 − 19 =

11) 12 − 7 =

12) 16 − 6 =

Subtraction

Answer the following Subtraction based questions.

1) 10 − 4 =

2) 10 − 2 =

3) 8 − 5 =

4) 14 − 7 =

5) 9 − 8 =

6) 17 − 5 =

7) 11 − 3 =

8) 13 − 12 =

9) 19 − 14 =

10) 18 − 5 =

11) 16 − 9 =

12) 9 − 3 =

Subtraction

Answer the following Subtraction based questions.

1) 15 − 2 =

2) 8 − 3 =

3) 20 − 12 =

4) 20 − 9 =

5) 20 − 18 =

6) 7 − 5 =

7) 15 − 8 =

8) 15 − 3 =

9) 17 − 6 =

10) 11 − 9 =

11) 7 − 4 =

12) 13 − 11 =

Subtraction

Count the number of pictures and subtract.

____ ____

____ ____

____ ____

Subtraction

Count the number of pictures and subtract.

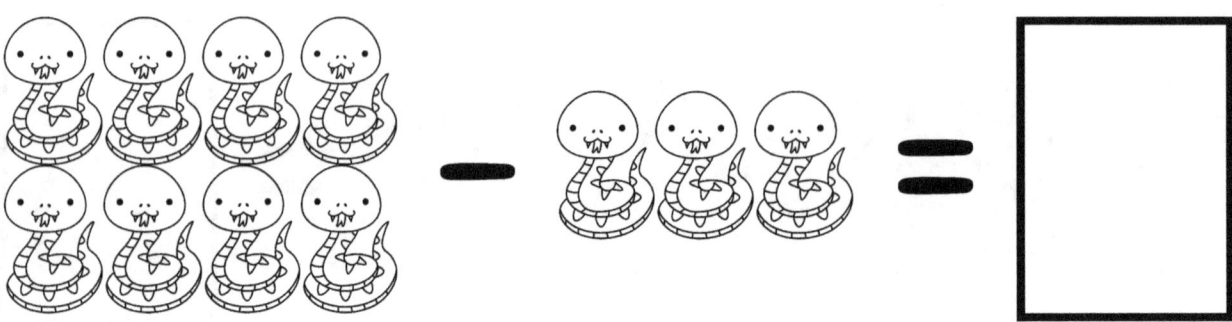

____   ____

____   ____

____   ____

Subtraction

Work out the answer to the following Subtraction based questions.

9 - 🐂🐂 = ☐

20 - 🏆🏆🏆🏆 = ☐

10 - 🧸🧸🧸 = ☐

Subtraction

Work out the answer to the following Subtraction based questions.

14 − 🐖🐖🐖🐖 = ☐

───

7 − 🦩 = ☐

───

19 − 🐙🐙🐙🐙🐙🐙 = ☐

───

Subtraction

Work out the answer to the following Subtraction based questions.

 − 5 = ☐

 − 3 = ☐

 − 7 = ☐

Subtraction

Work out the answer to the following Subtraction based questions.

 − 8 = ☐

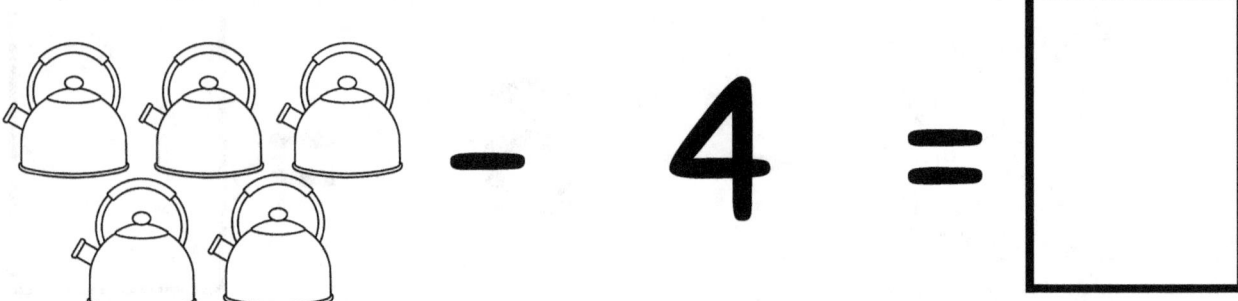 − 4 = ☐

 − 3 = ☐

Subtraction

Work out the answer to the following Subtraction based questions.

There are 5 pumpkins in the patch. If you pick 2 pumpkins, how many are left?

_____

There are 20 lizards sitting on a rock. 8 lizards crawl away.
How many lizards are left on the rock?

_____

There are 7 horses in a field. 3 horses walk away. How many horses are left in the field?

_____

Subtraction

Work out the answer to the following Subtraction based questions.

You have 5 burgers on a plate. You eat 2 burgers. How many burgers are left on the plate?

_____

There are 20 lizards sitting on a rock. 8 lizards crawl away. How many lizards are left on the rock?

_____

There are 20 cows in the field. 14 cows go back to the barn. How many cows are left in the field?

_____

Before

Fill in the number before 12.

_____ **12 13**

Fill in the number before 7.

_____ **7 8**

Fill in the number before 11.

_____ **11 12**

Fill in the number before 19.

_____ **19 20**

Before

Fill in the number before 9

_____   9   10

Fill in the number before 13.

_____   13   14

Fill in the number before 6.

_____   6   7

Fill in the number before 17.

_____   17   18

After

Fill in the number after 9.

8   9   _____

Fill in the number after 13.

12   13   _____

Fill in the number after 6.

5   6   _____

Fill in the number after 19.

18   19   _____

After

Fill in the number after 3.

2   3   _____

Fill in the number after 12.

11   12   _____

Fill in the number after 16.

15   16   _____

Fill in the number after 5.

4   5   _____

Between

Fill in the number between 11 and 13.

11 _____ 13

Fill in the number between 2 and 4.

2 _____ 4

Fill in the number between 17 and 19.

17 _____ 19

Fill in the number between 15 and 17.

15 _____ 17

Between

Fill in the number between 9 and 11.

9 _____ 11

Fill in the number between 10 and 12.

10 _____ 12

Fill in the number between 18 and 20.

18 _____ 20

Fill in the number between 14 and 16.

14 _____ 16

Missing Numbers

Fill in the Missing Numbers.

1	3	5	7	9	11
☐	15	☐	19	21	23
25	27	29	31	☐	35
☐	☐	41	43	45	47
☐	51	53	☐	57	59
☐	63	☐	67	69	☐

Missing Numbers

Fill in the Missing Numbers.

71	73	75	77	☐	81
83	☐	87	89	91	93
95	97	99	101	☐	☐
107	☐	111	113	☐	117
☐	121	123	☐	127	129
☐	133	135	137	139	☐

Missing Numbers

Fill in the Missing Numbers.

1	2	3	☐	☐	6	☐	☐	☐	10
☐	12	13	14	15	16	17	☐	☐	20
☐	22	23	24	25	26	☐	28	29	30
31	32	33	☐	35	☐	37	38	39	☐
41	42	43	☐	45	46	47	48	49	50
51	52	53	☐	☐	☐	57	58	59	☐
61	62	63	64	65	66	67	☐	☐	70
71	72	73	74	75	☐	77	78	79	☐
81	82	83	☐	85	☐	87	☐	☐	90
☐	92	93	94	95	96	97	98	99	☐

Missing Numbers

Fill in the Missing Numbers.

	101	102			105		107	108	109
110		112	113	114	115	116	117	118	
120	121	122	123	124				128	129
		132		134	135	136	137	138	139
140			143	144	145	146	147	148	149
150		152	153	154	155	156			
	161	162	163	164	165		167		
	171	172	173		175		177	178	
180	181	182	183	184	185	186	187	188	189
190		192	193	194	195		197	198	199

Missing Numbers

Work out the pattern of Missing Numbers and write them down.

	16		20	
24		28		32
	36		40	
44		48		52
	56		60	

Missing Numbers

Work out the pattern of Missing Numbers and write them down.

	25		35	
45		55		65
	75		85	
95		105		115
	125		135	

Missing Numbers

Work out the pattern of Missing Numbers and write them down.

	30		50	
70		90		110
	130		150	
170		190		210
	230		250	

Odd Vs Even

Write underneath the number if it is Odd or Even.

12   9

_____ _____

19   15

_____ _____

16   6

_____ _____

Odd Vs Even

Write underneath the number if it is Odd or Even.

5	8
_____	_____

20	17
_____	_____

13	10
_____	_____

Odd Vs Even

Write if the amount of pictures in each box is Odd or Even.

_____

_____

_____

Odd Vs Even

Write if the amount of pictures in each box is Odd or Even.

Counting

Count how many of each picture and write in boxes at the bottom.

Counting

Count how many of each picture and write in boxes at the bottom.

Counting

Count how many of each picture and write in boxes at the bottom.

Counting

Count how many of each picture and circle the corret number.

1)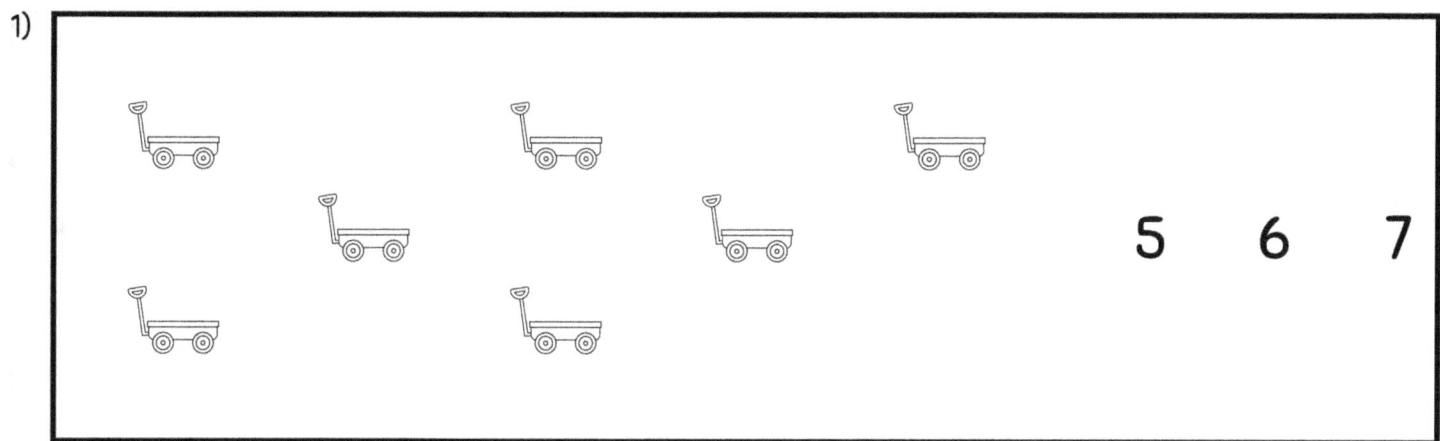
   5   6   7

2)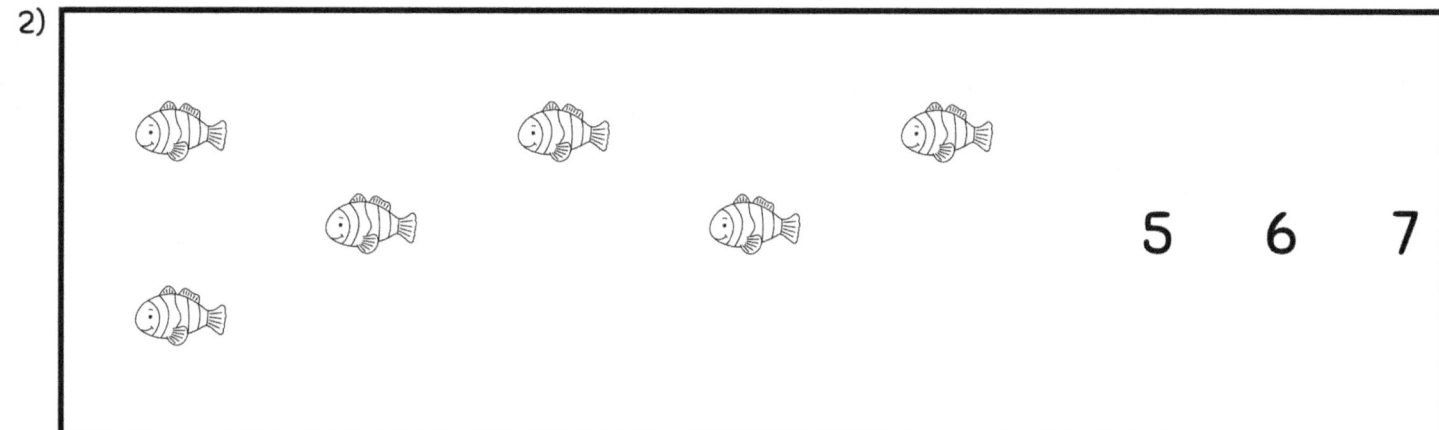
   5   6   7

3)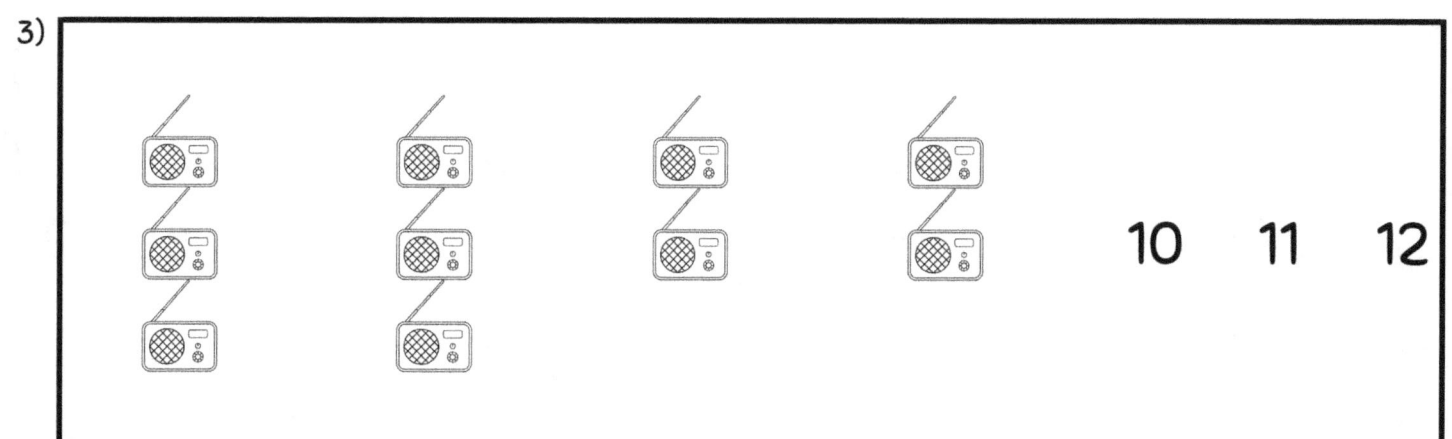
   10   11   12

Counting

Count how many of each picture and circle the corret number.

1)   7   8   9

2)   8   9   10

3)   7   8   9

Counting

Count how many of each picture and circle the corret number.

1)

10   11   12

2)

10   11   12

3)

10   11   12

Left Vs Right

Color the picture on the left.

Color the picture on the right.

Color the picture on the left.

Color the picture on the right.

Left Vs Right

Color the picture on the right.

Color the picture on the right.

Color the picture on the left.

Color the picture on the left.

Left Vs Right

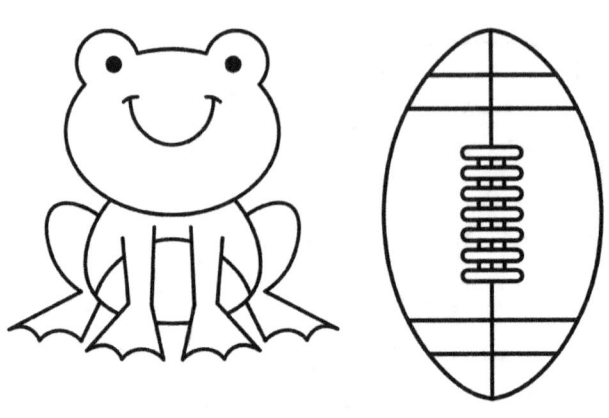

Color the picture on the left.

Color the picture on the left.

Color the picture on the right.

Color the picture on the right.

Left Vs Right

Color the picture on the left.

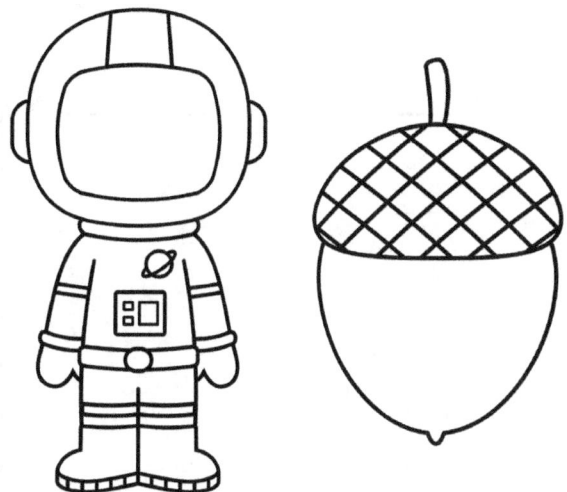

Color the picture on the left.

Color the picture on the right.

Color the picture on the right.

Heavy Vs Light

Circle the object which is lighter in weight in each box

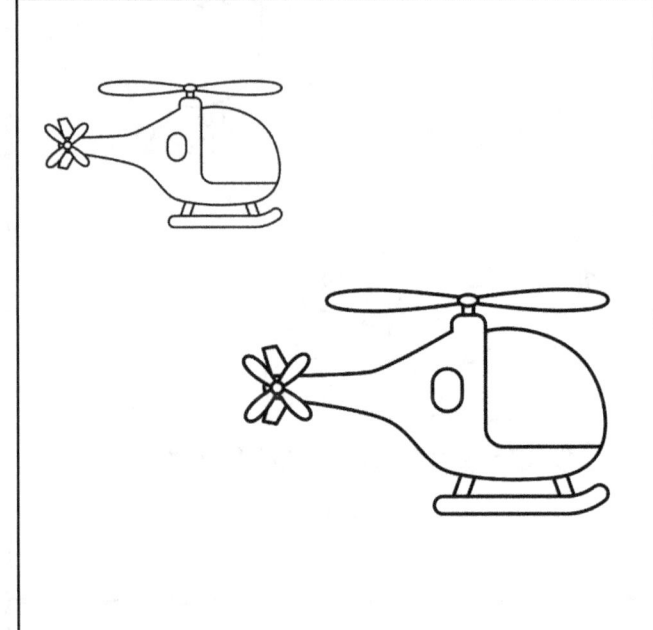

Heavy Vs Light

Circle the object which is lighter in weight in each box

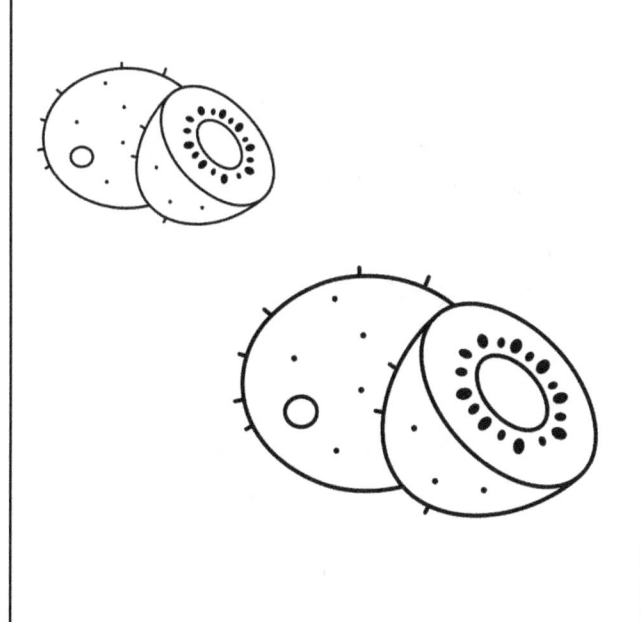

Heavy Vs Light

Circle the object which is heavier in weight in each box

Heavy Vs Light

Circle the object which is heavier in weight in each box

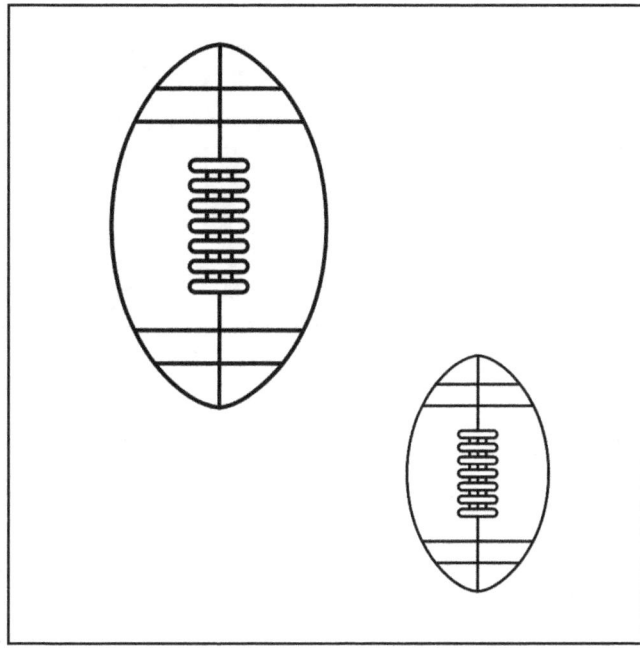

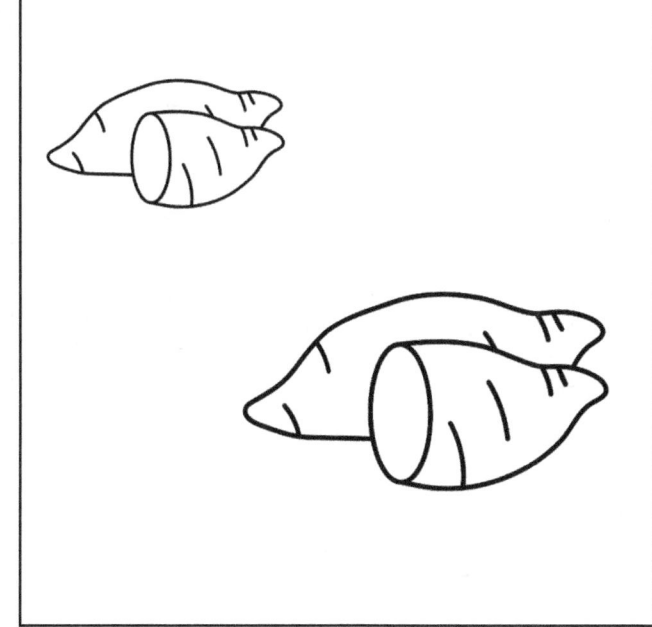

Heavy Vs Light

Put the below object in weight order. With 1 being the lightest, and 3 being the heaviest.

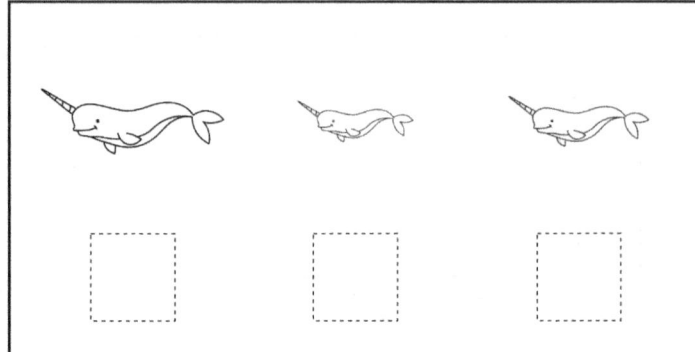

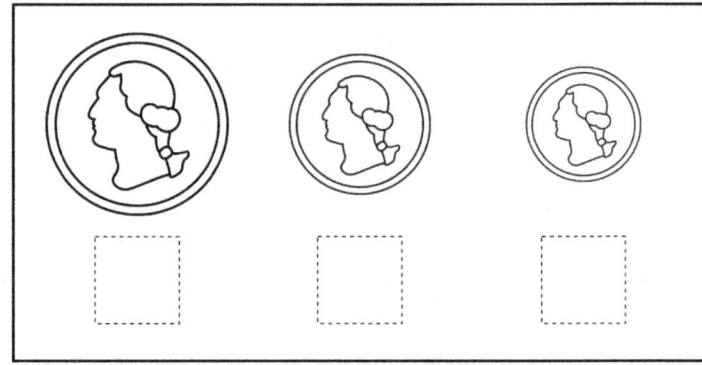

Heavy Vs Light

Put the below object in weight order. With 1 being the lightest, and 3 being the heaviest.

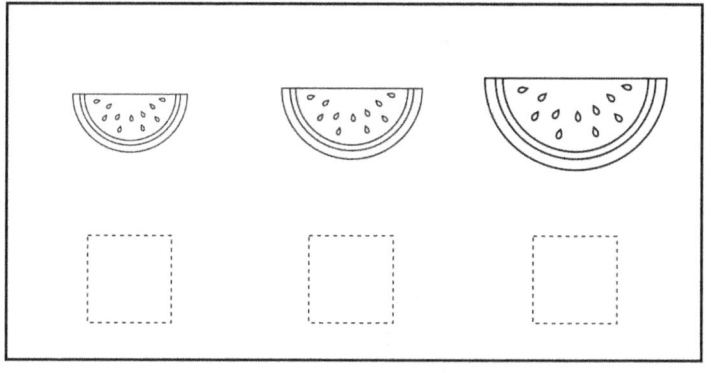

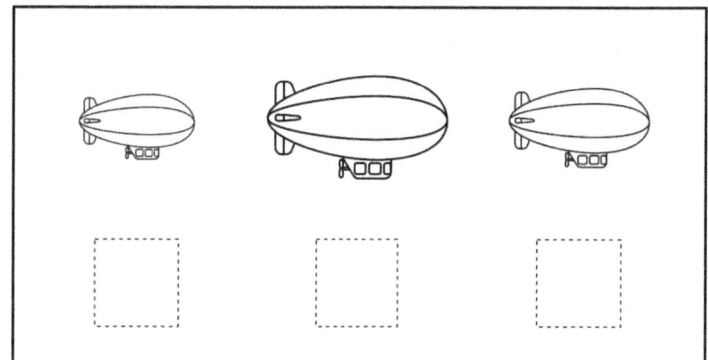

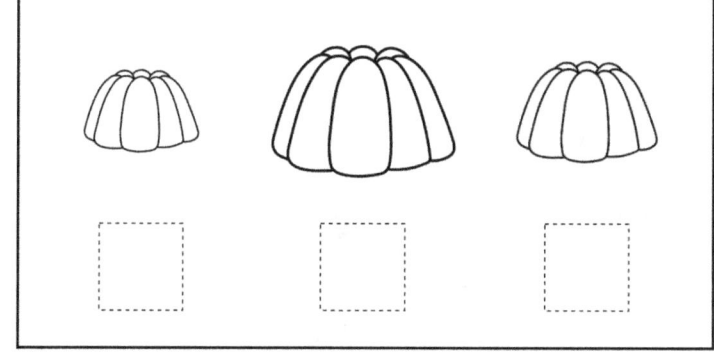

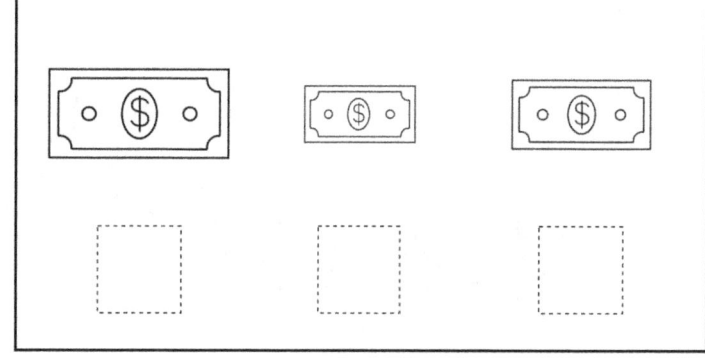

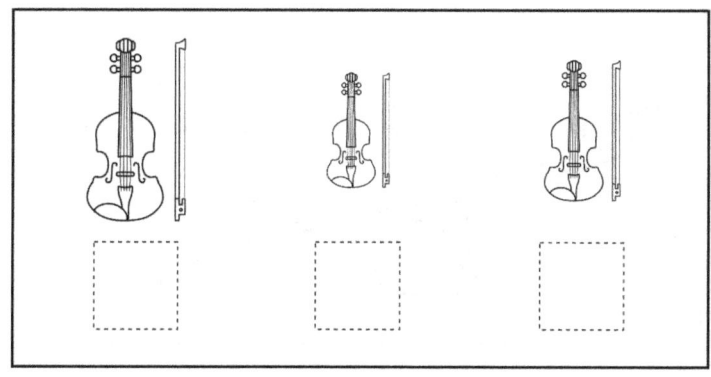

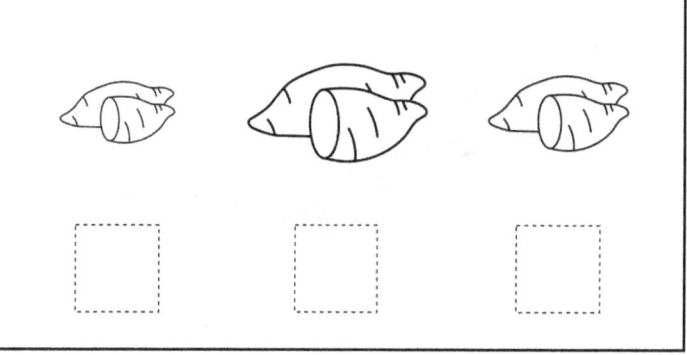

Heavy Vs Light

Look at each seesaw and circle which object is shown as being the lightest.

Heavy Vs Light

Look at each seesaw and circle which object is shown as being the lightest.

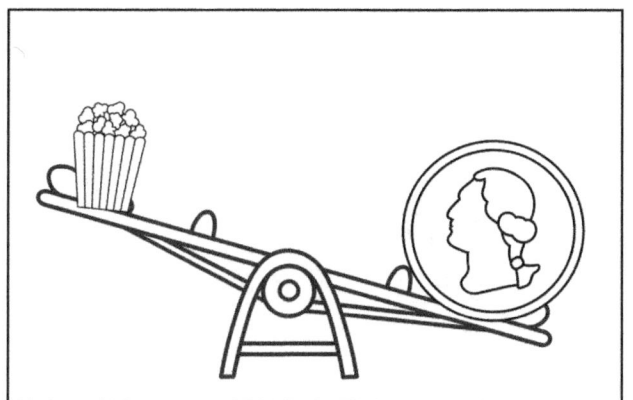

Heavy Vs Light

Look at each seesaw and circle which object is shown as being the heaviest.

Heavy Vs Light

Look at each seesaw and circle which object is shown as being the heaviest.

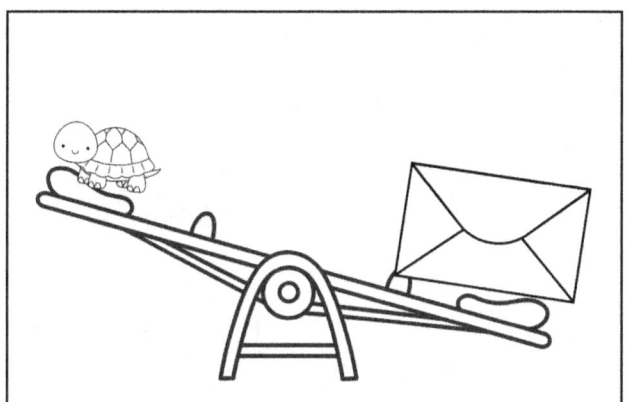

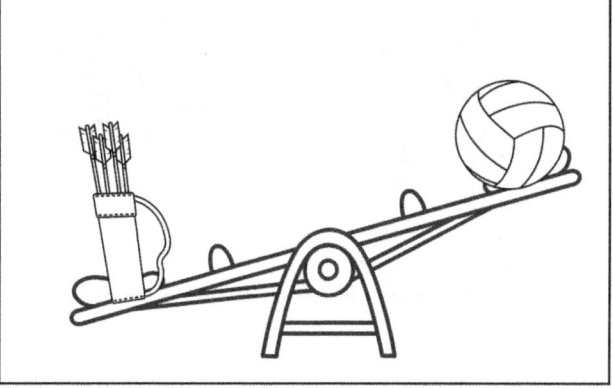

More Vs Less

Count the number of each picture and write down to see which is more and which is less.

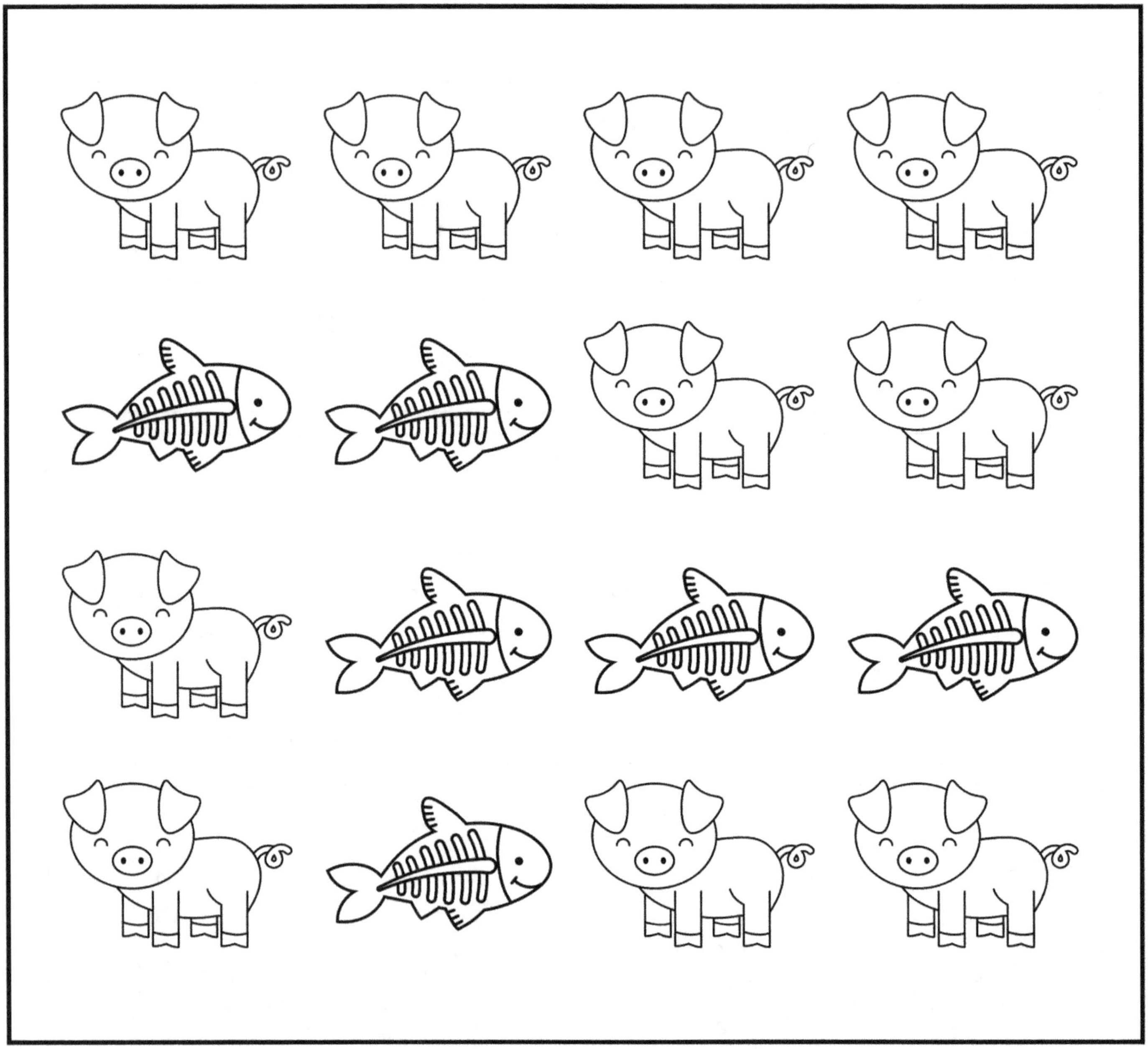

More Vs Less

Count the number of each picture and write down to see which is more and which is less.

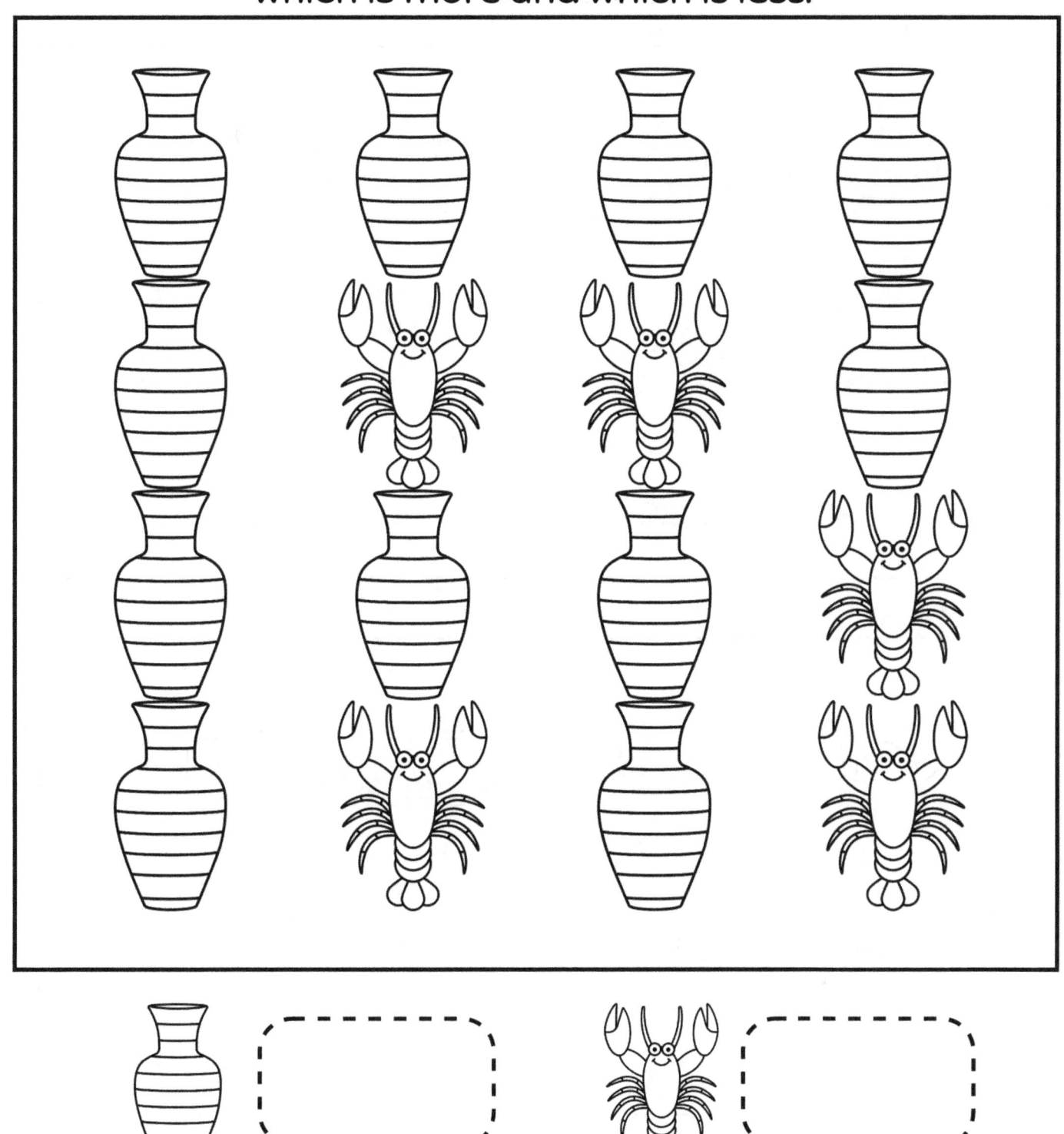

More Vs Less

Count the number of each picture and write down to see which is more and which is less.

1)
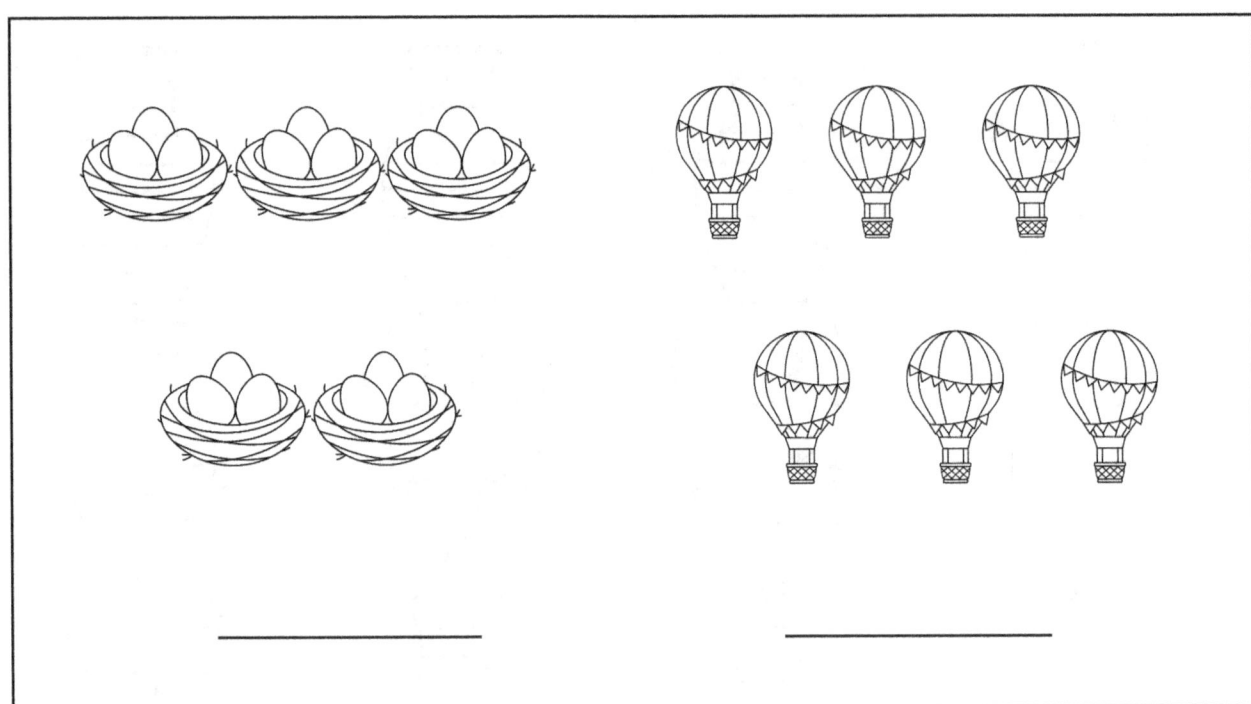

_____   _____

2)
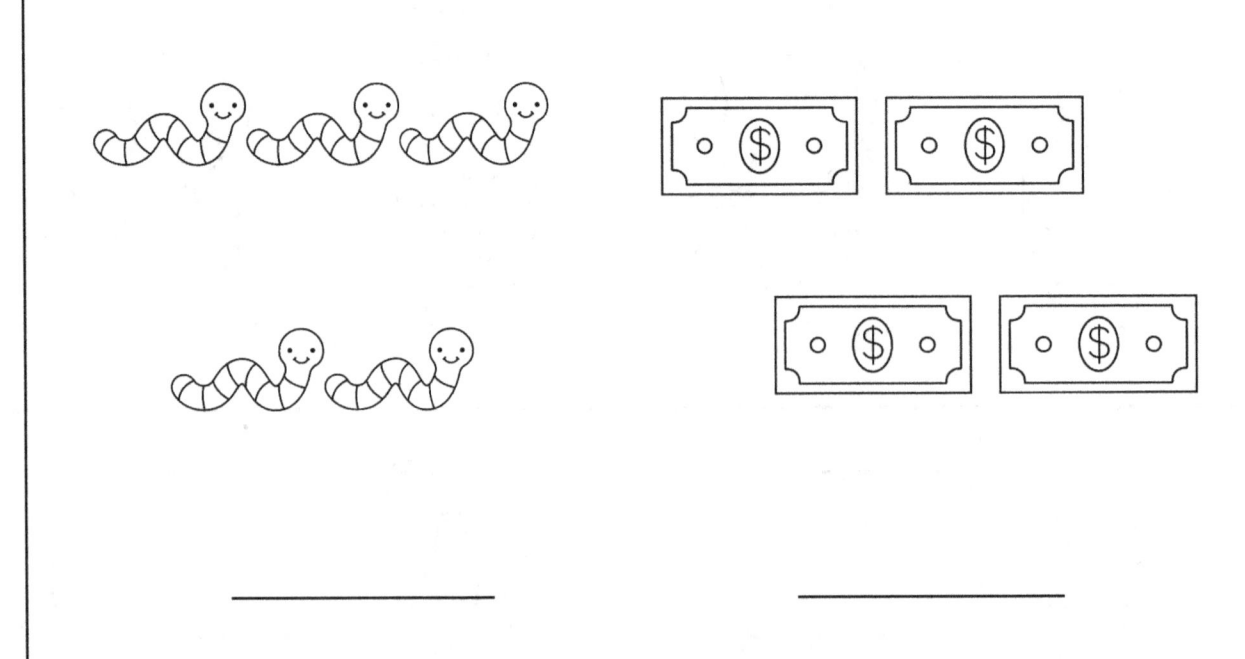

_____   _____

More Vs Less

Count the number of each picture and write down to see which is more and which is less.

1)

_____   _____

2)

_____   _____

More Vs Less

Count the number of each picture and write down to see which is more and which is less.

1)

2)

Capacity

Look at the jugs below and write the capacity for each

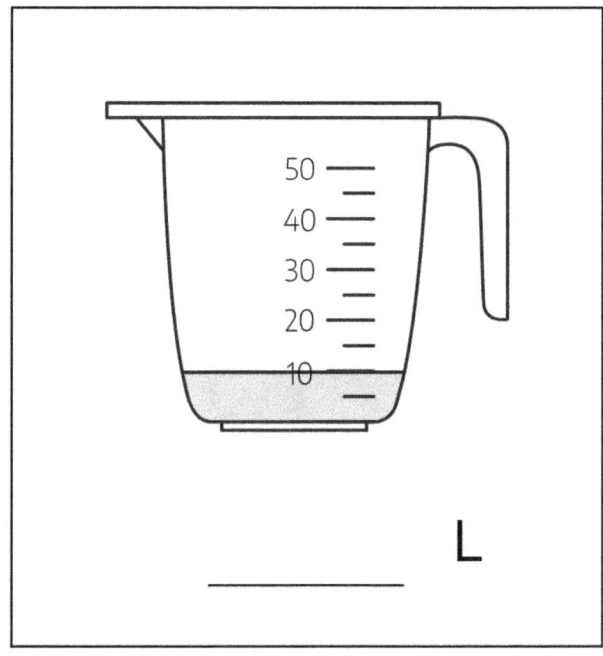

L
_____

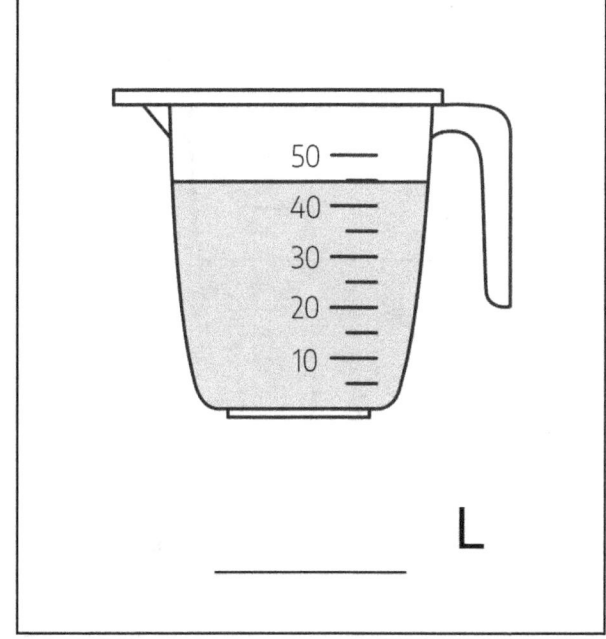

L
_____

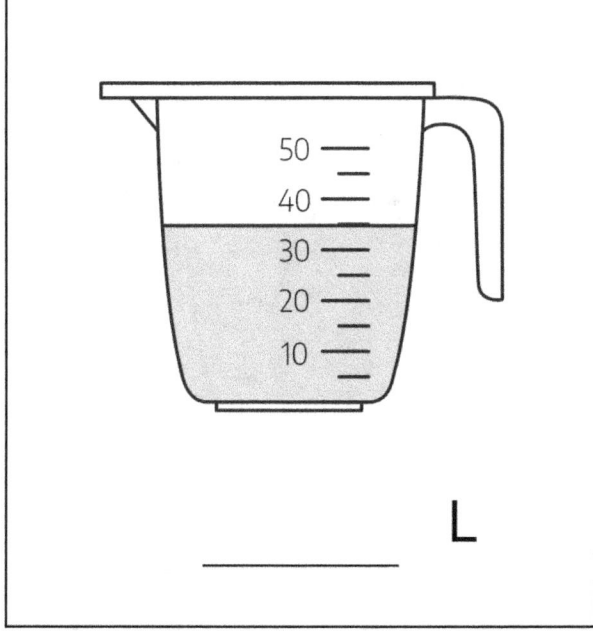

L
_____

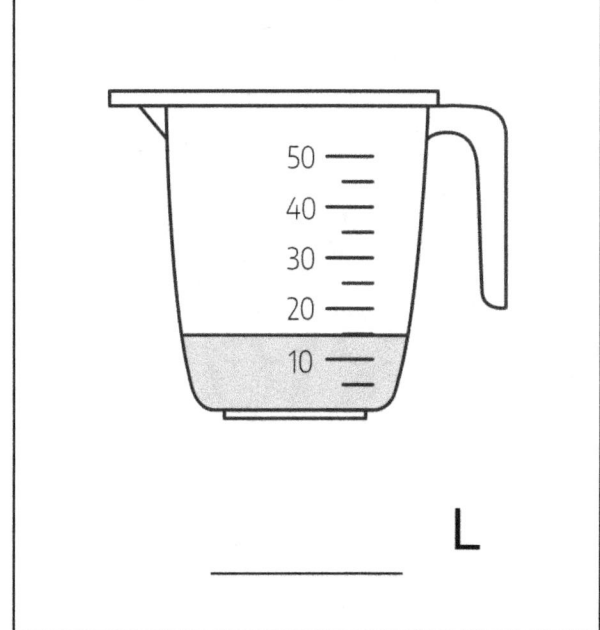

L
_____

Capacity

Look at the jugs below and write the capacity for each

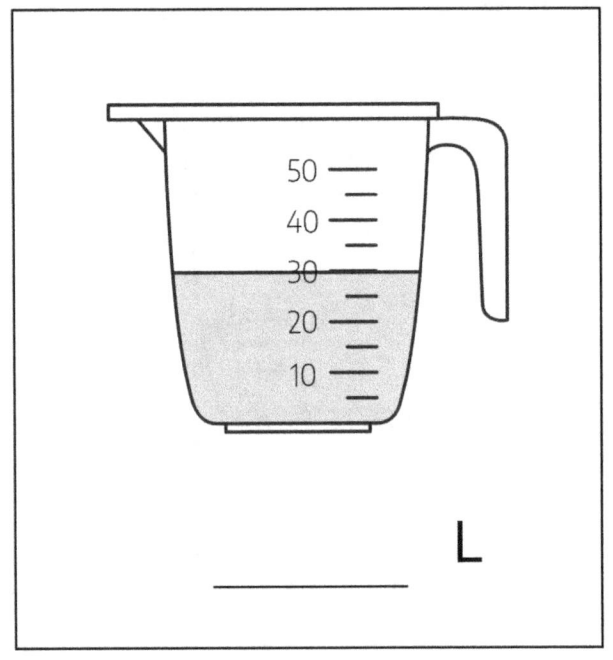

_____ L

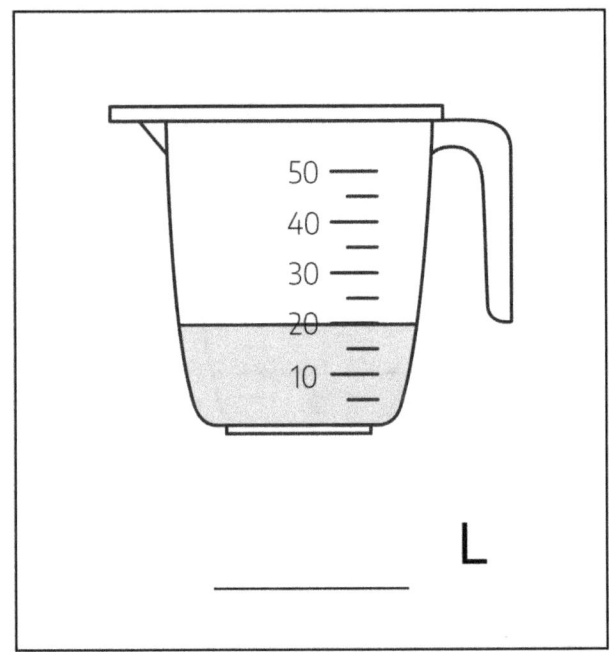

_____ L

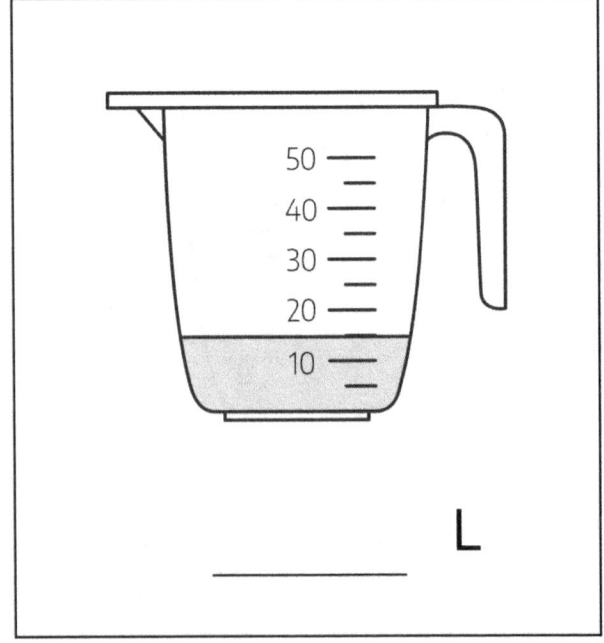

_____ L

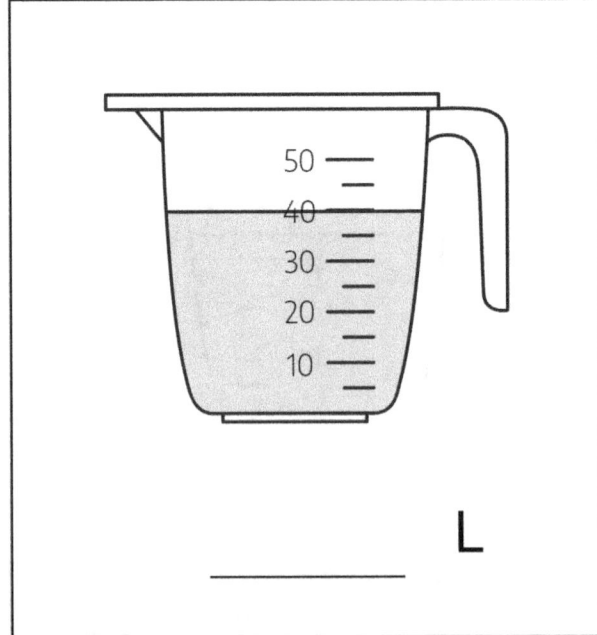

_____ L

Capacity

Shade in the capacity of jugs to match the capacity shown..

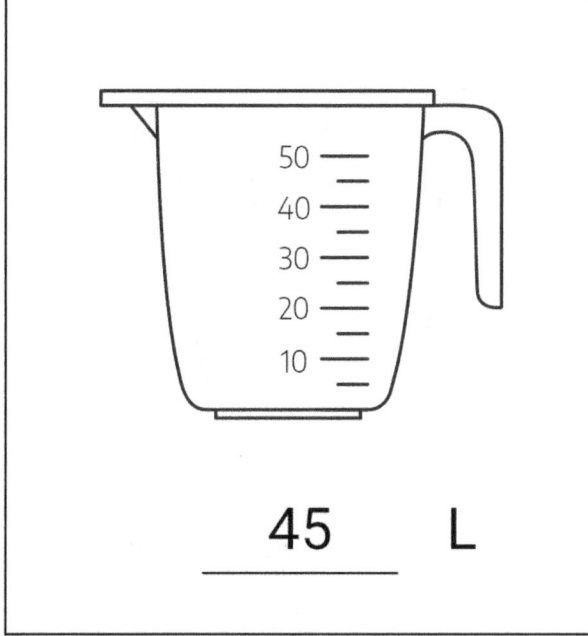

45 _____ L

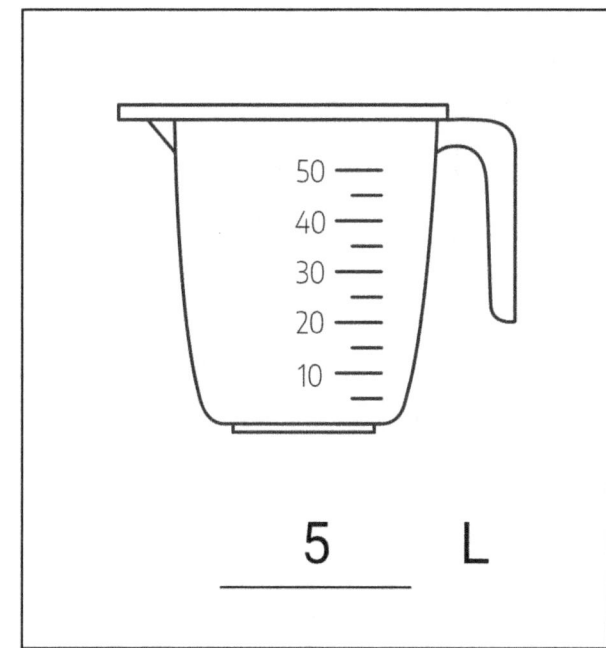

5 _____ L

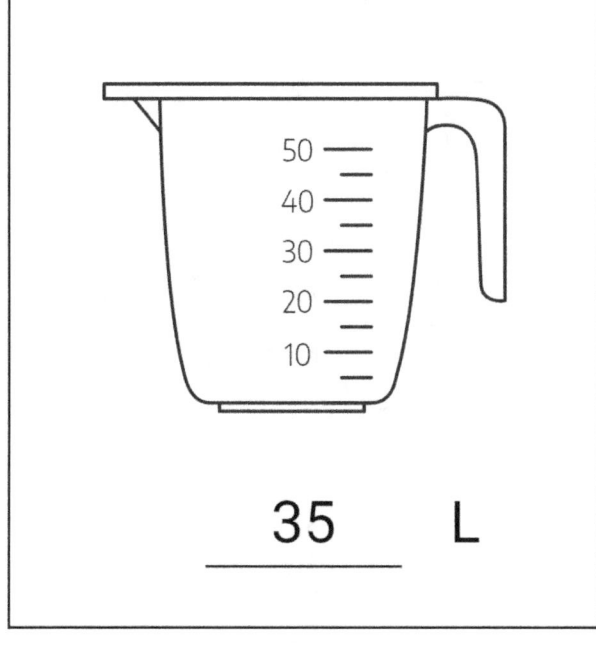

35 _____ L

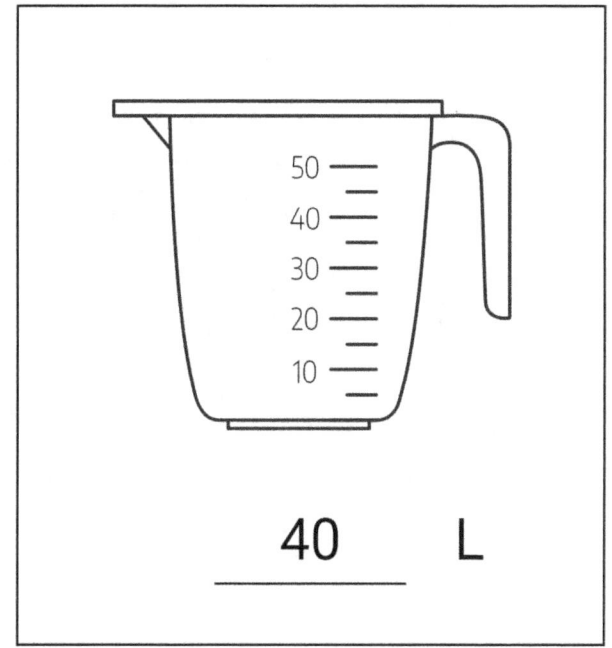

40 _____ L

Capacity

Shade in the capacity of jugs to match the capacity shown..

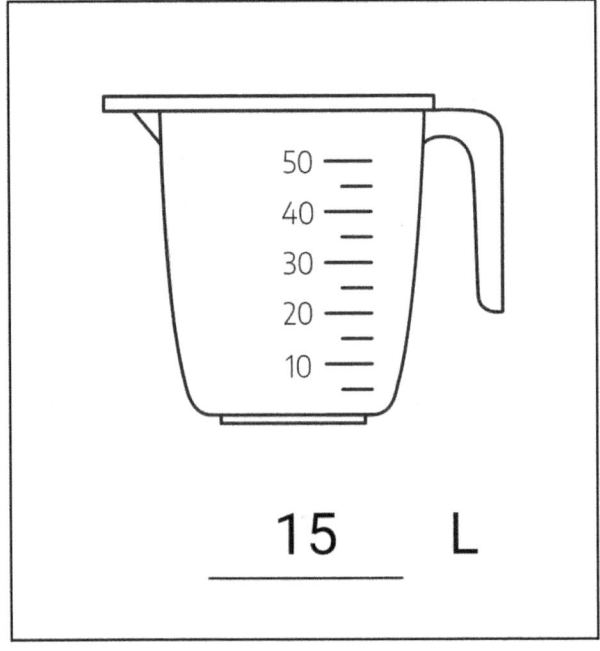

15   L

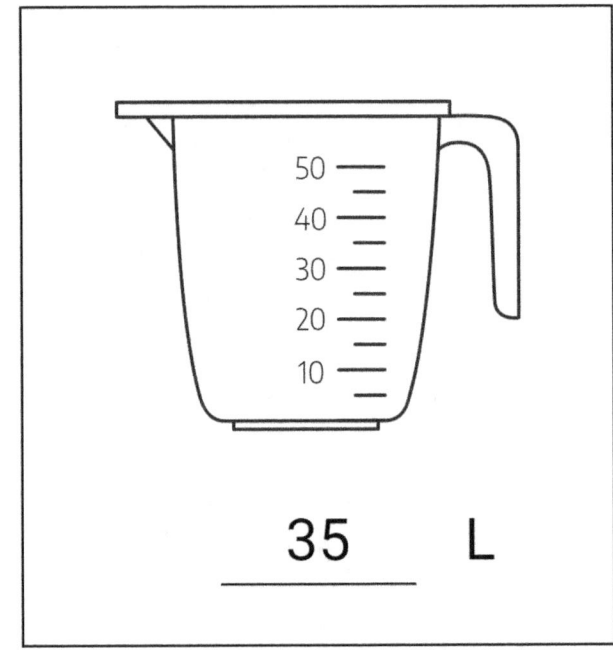

35   L

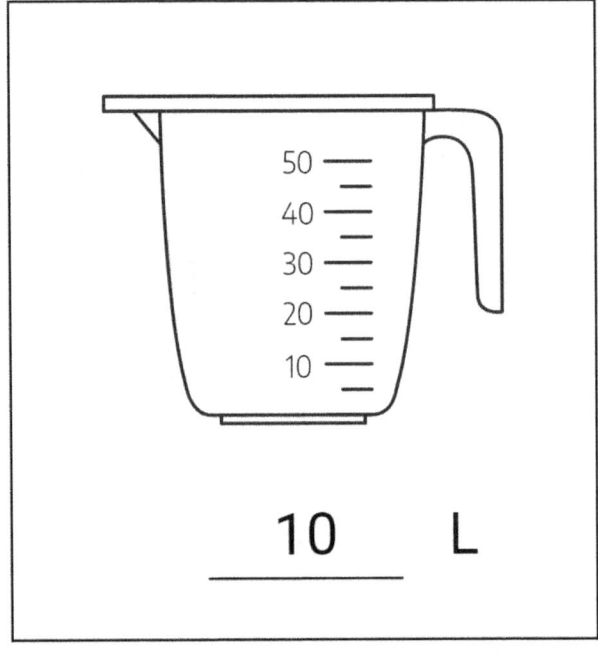

10   L

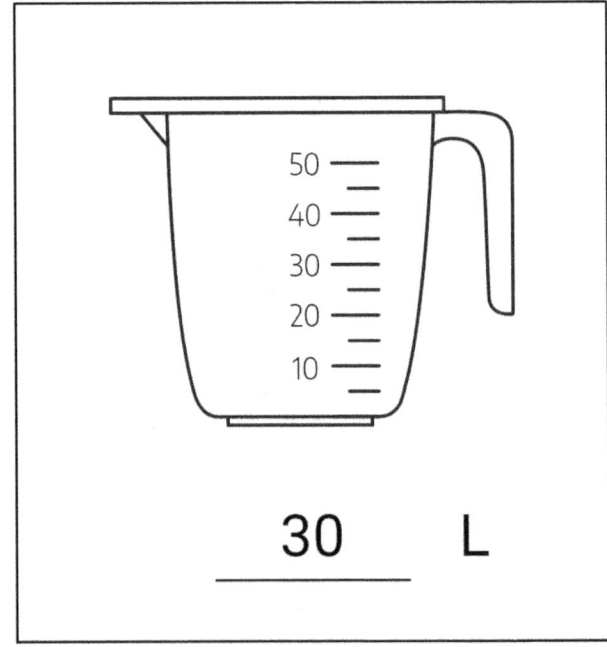

30   L

Capacity

Write down the capacity of each to jug to find out which is holding more.

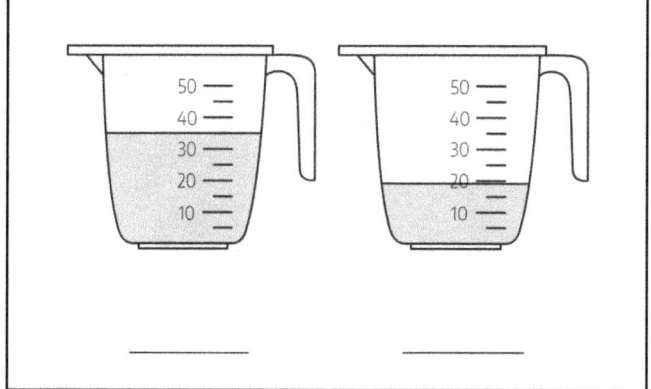

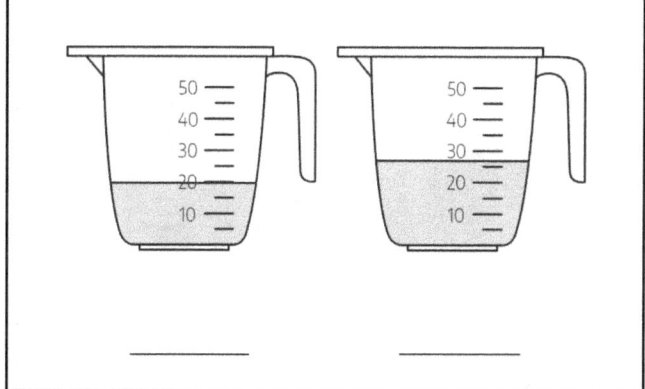

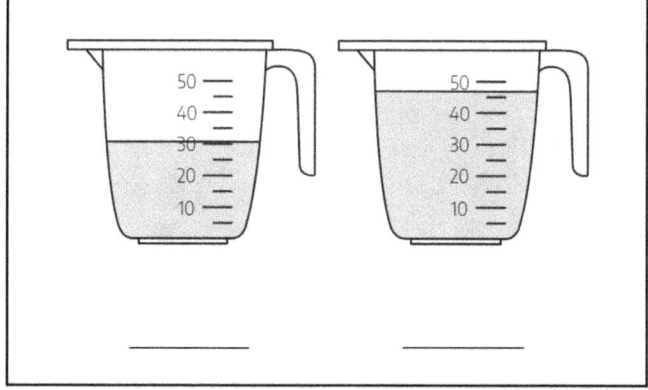

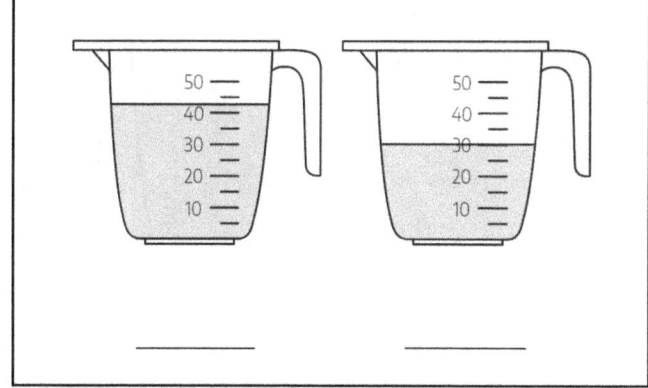

Capacity

Write down the capacity of each to jug to find out which is holding more.

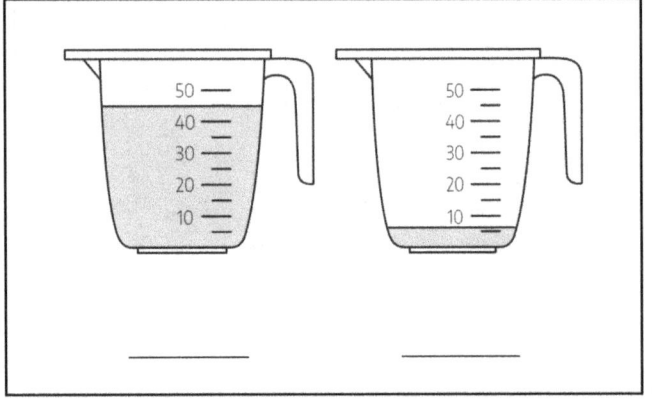 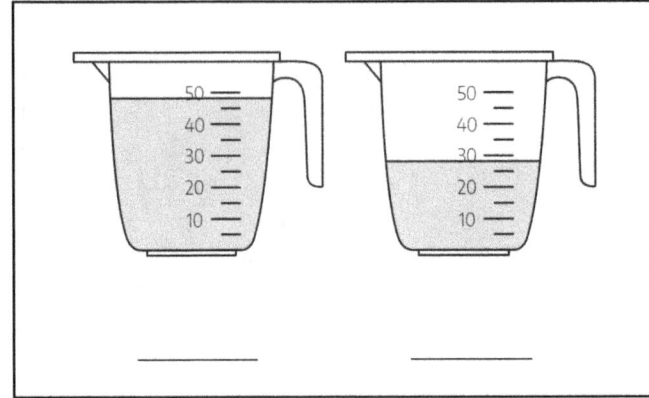

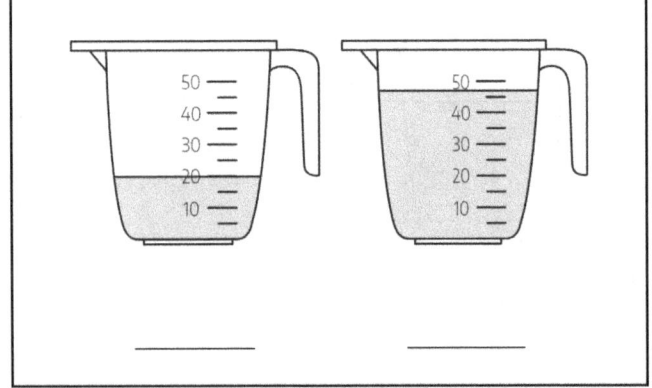 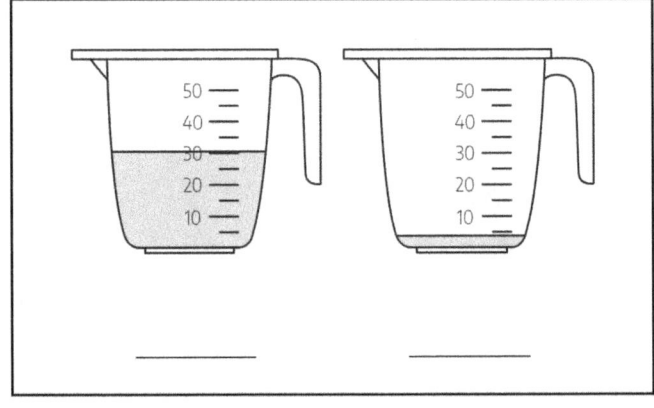

Temperature

Look at the temperature gauge and write the temperature below it.

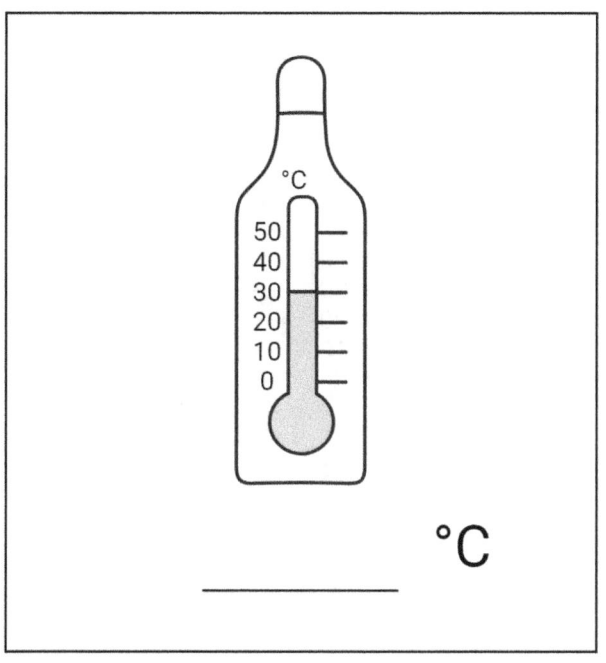

_____ °C

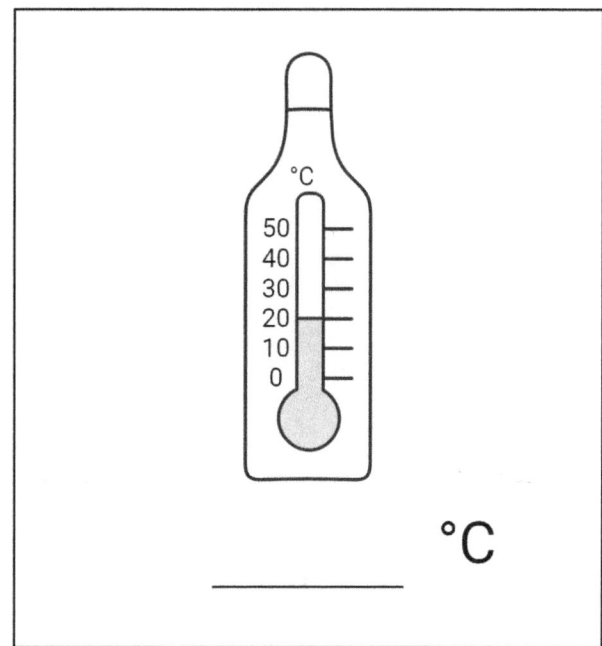

_____ °C

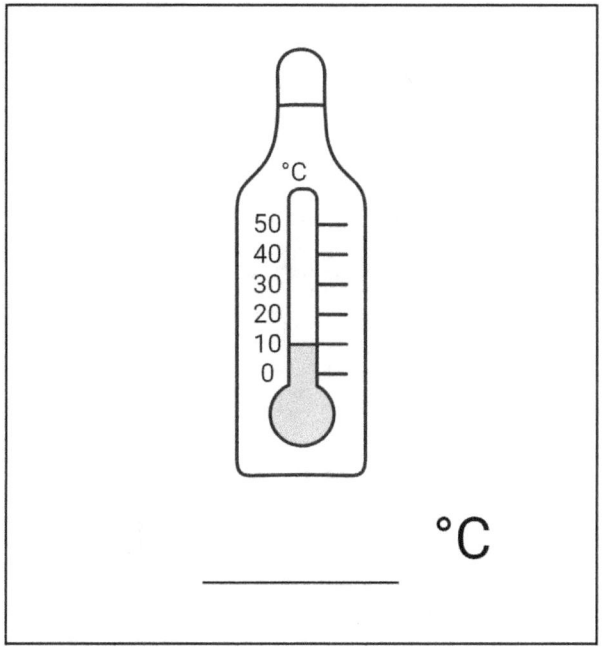

_____ °C

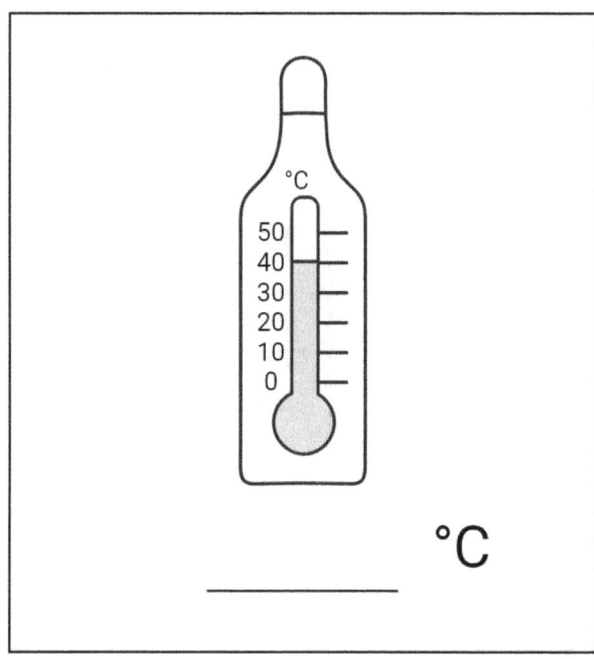

_____ °C

Temperature

Look at the temperature gauge and write the temperature below it.

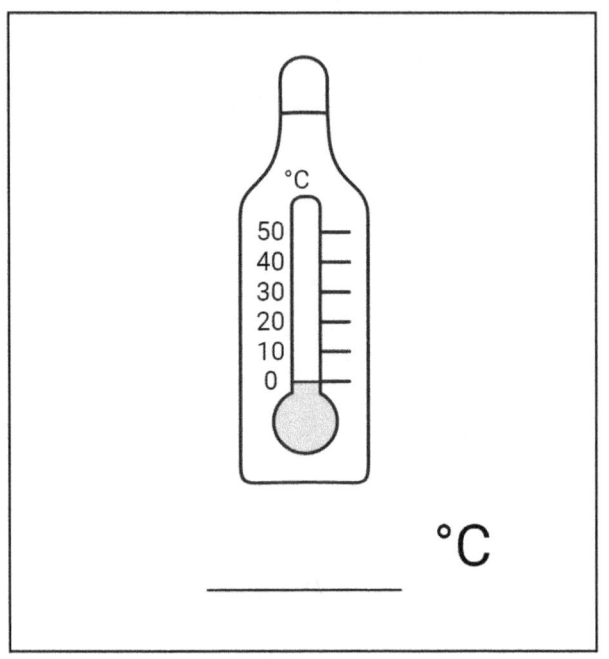

_____ °C

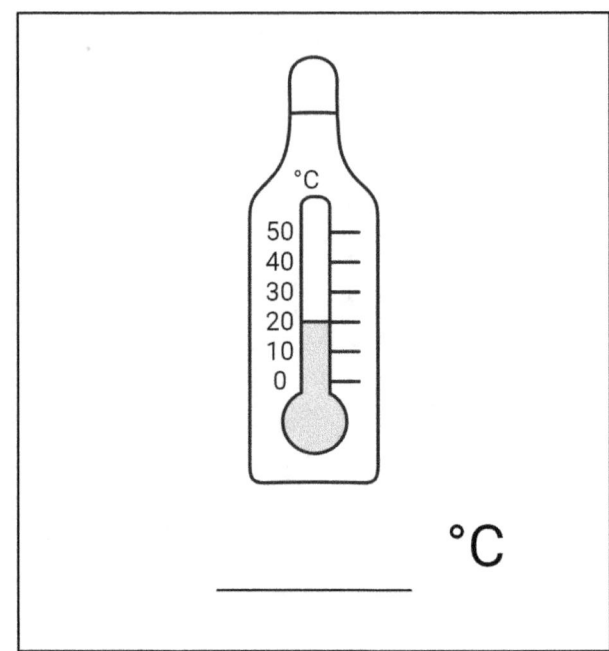

_____ °C

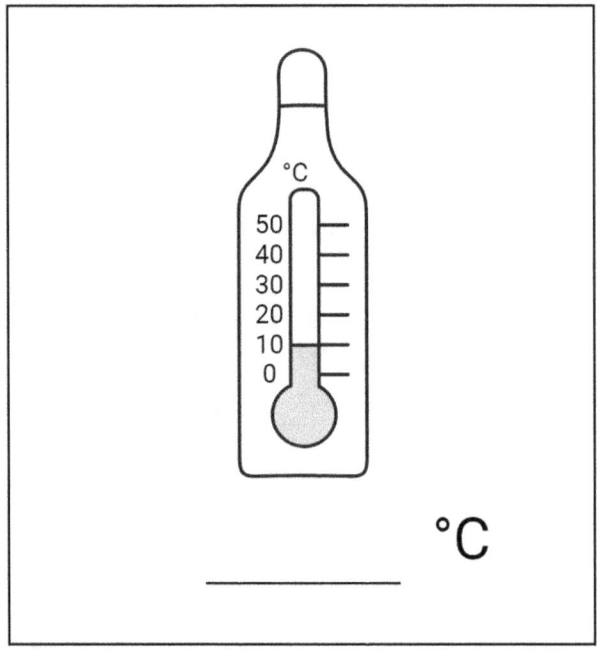

_____ °C

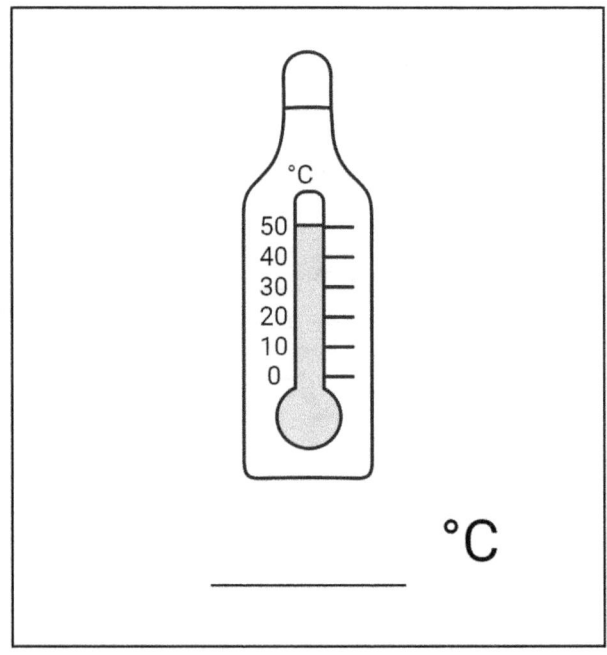

_____ °C

Temperature

Look at the temperature written and shade in the temperature gauge to match it.

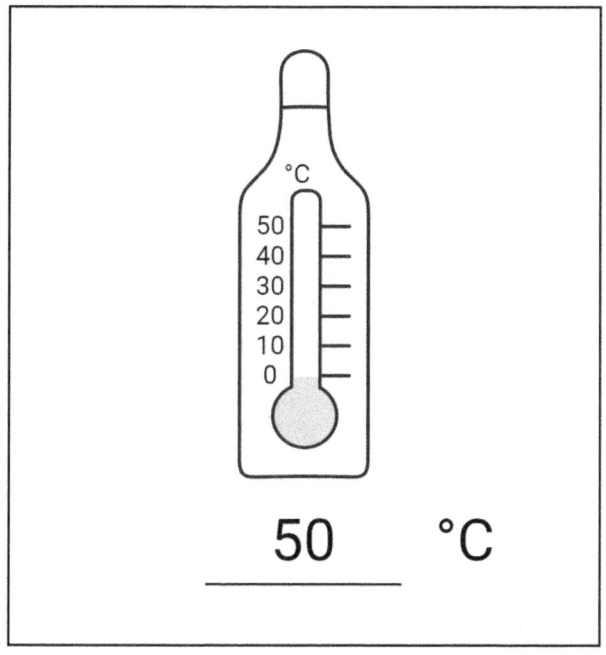

50 °C

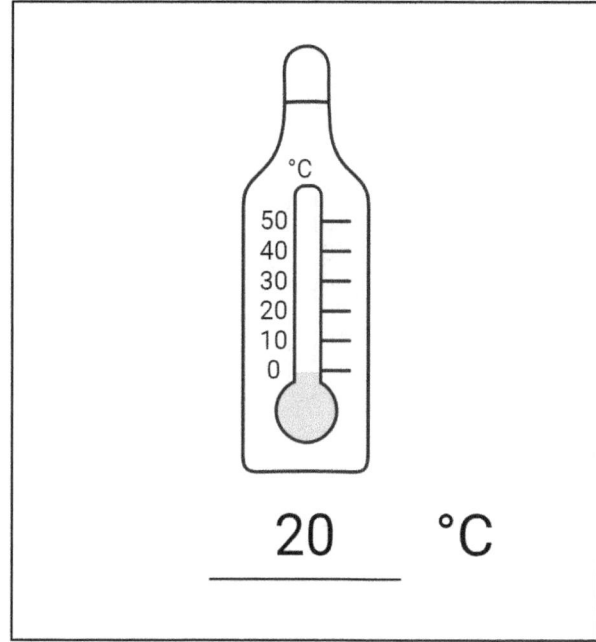

20 °C

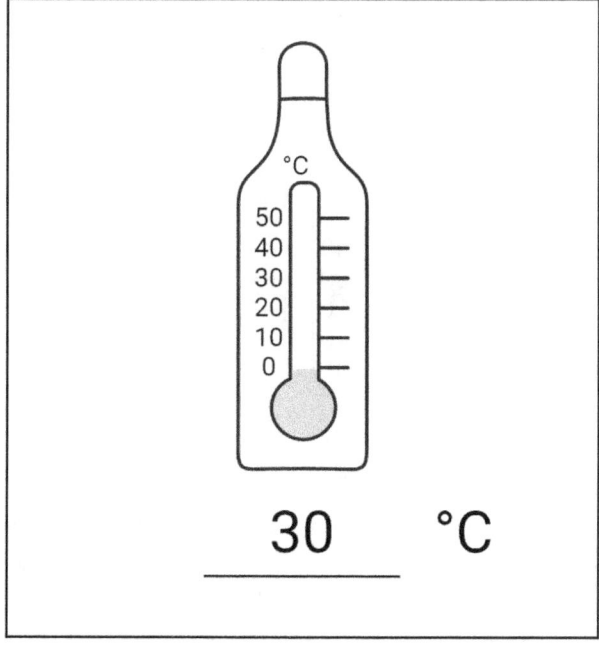

30 °C

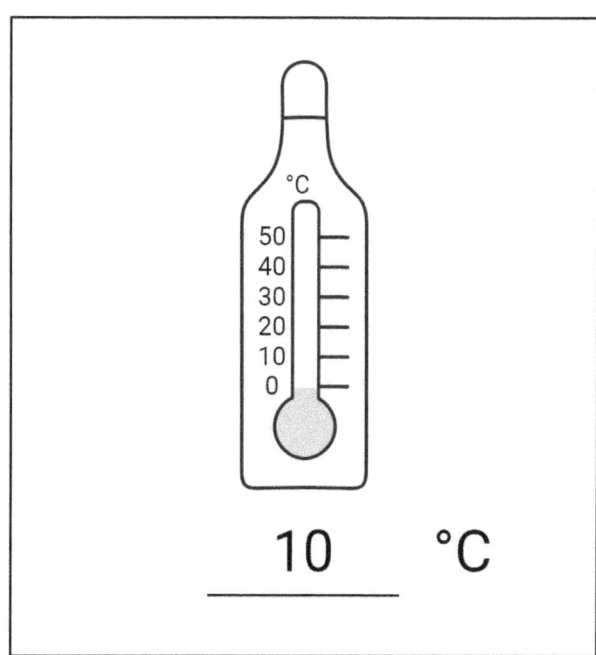

10 °C

Temperature

Look at the temperature written and shade in the temperature gauge to match it.

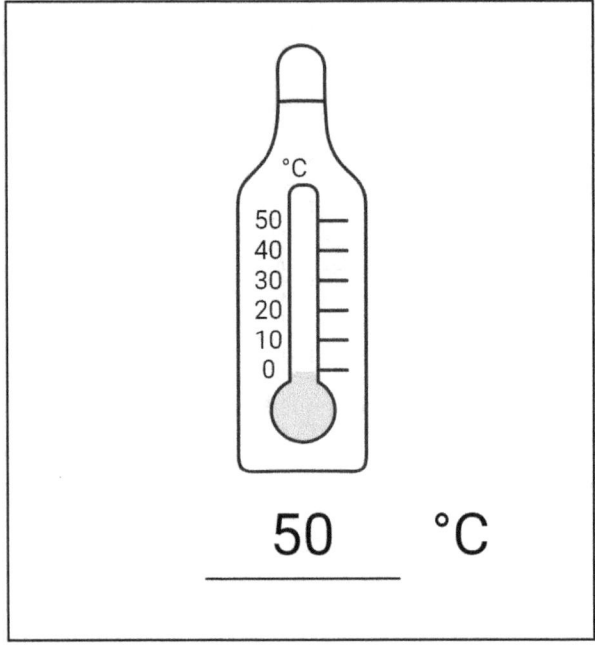

50 °C

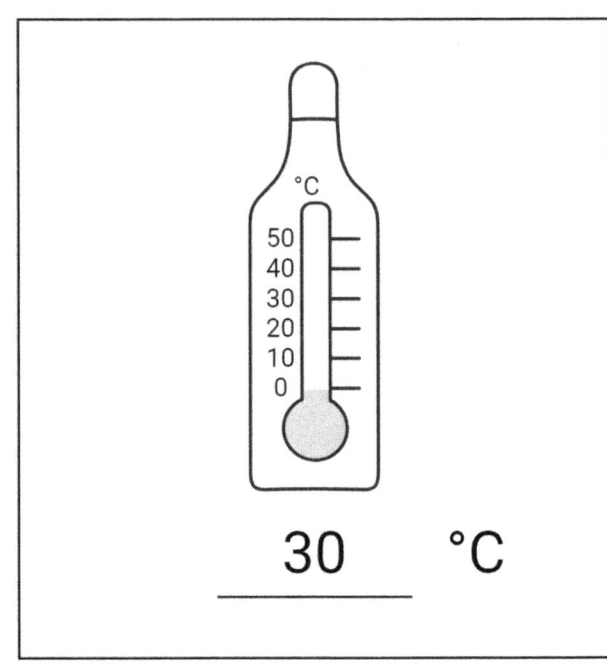

30 °C

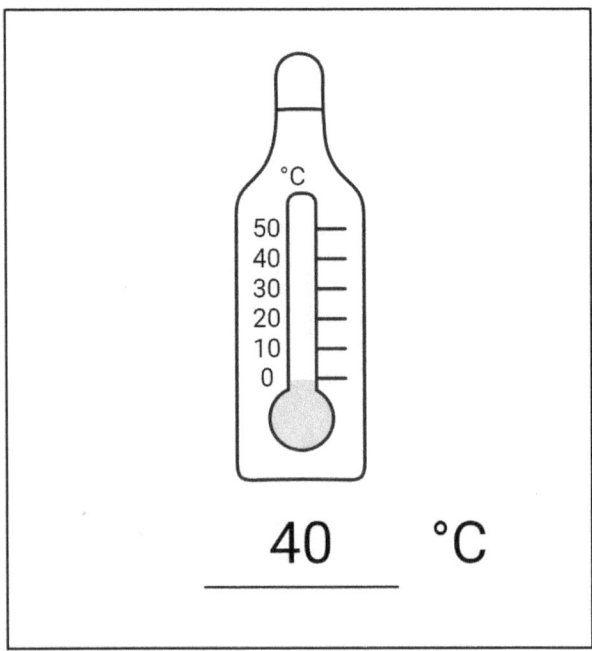

40 °C

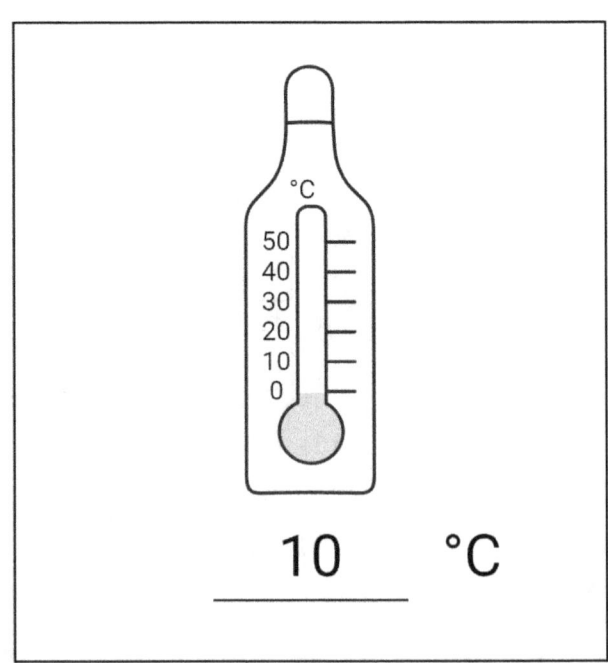

10 °C

Temperature

Look at the temperature gauges and write underneath which one is hotter and which is colder.

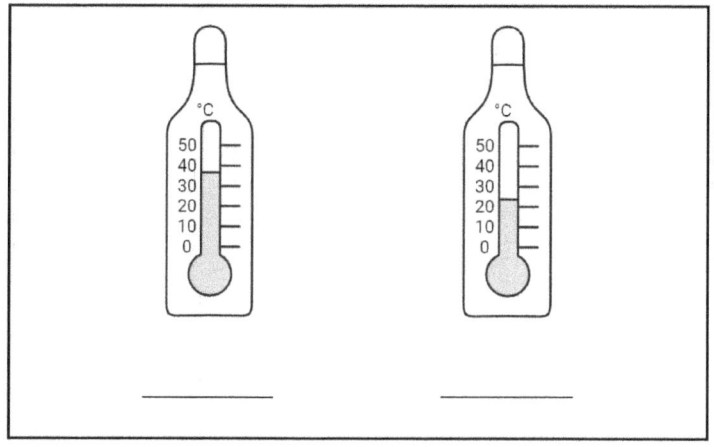

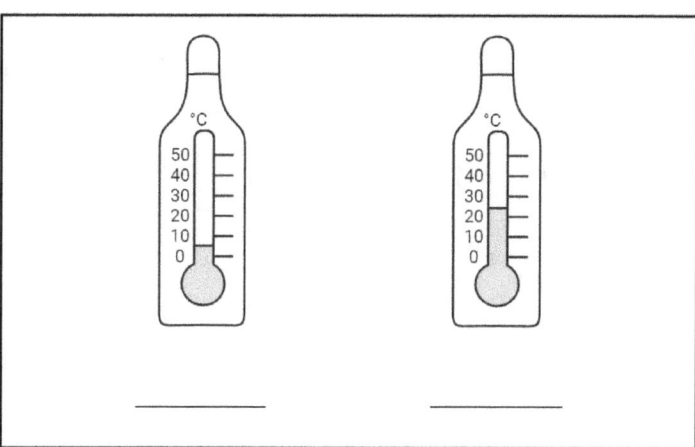

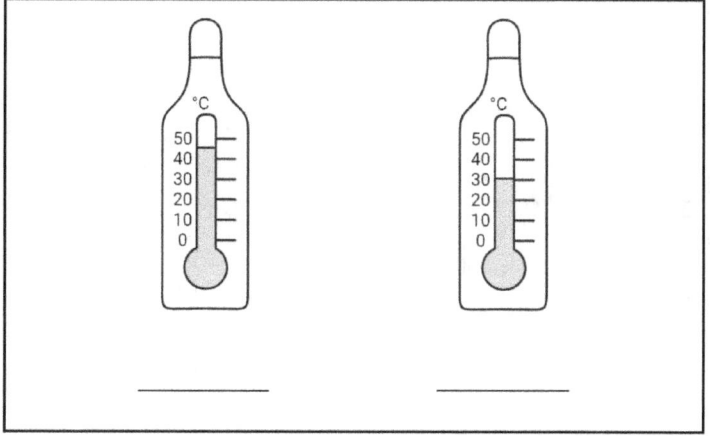

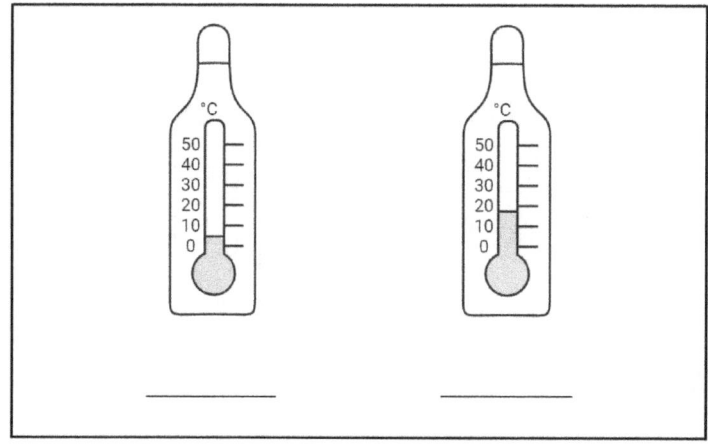

Temperature

Look at the temperature gauges and write underneath which one is hotter and which is colder.

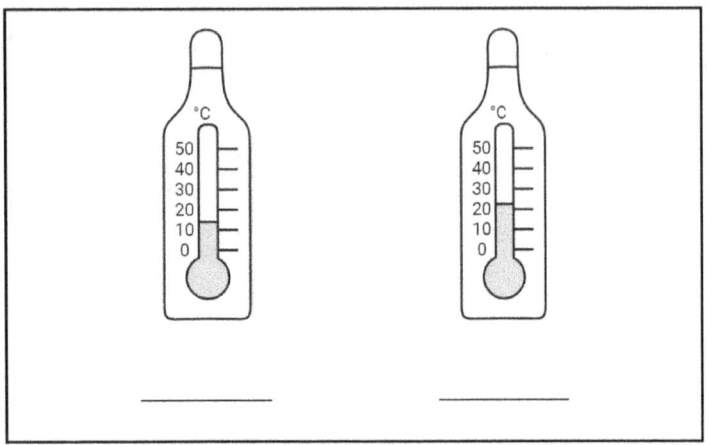

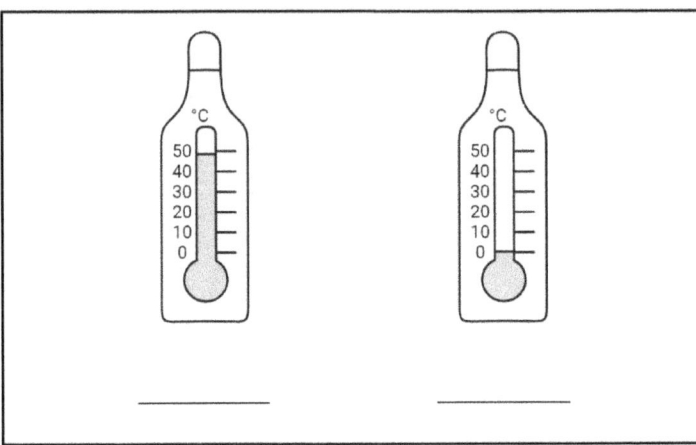

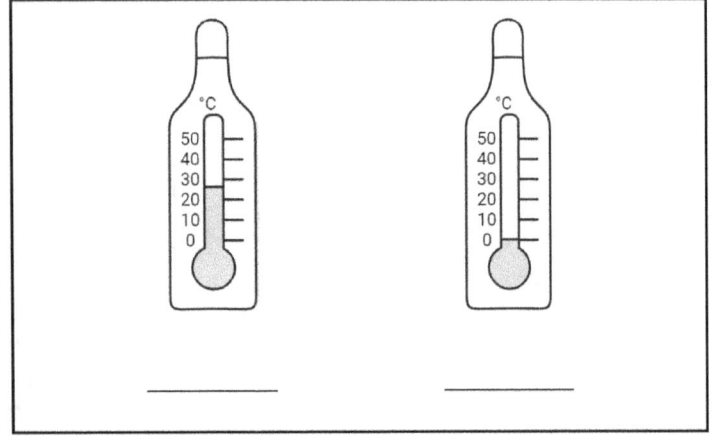

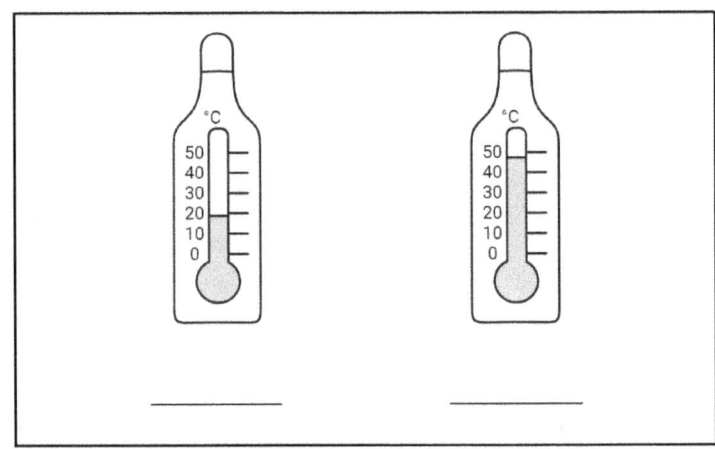

Time

Look at the clock faces below and enter the correct time.

1)
___ o'clock

2)
___ o'clock

3)
___ o'clock

4)
___ o'clock

5)
___ o'clock

6)
___ o'clock

7)
___ o'clock

8)
___ o'clock

9)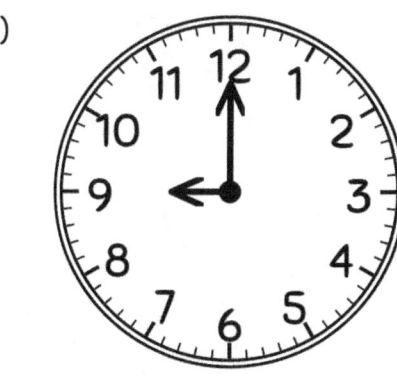
___ o'clock

Time

Look at the clock faces below and enter the correct time.

1)
___ o'clock

2)
___ o'clock

3)
___ o'clock

4)
___ o'clock

5)
___ o'clock

6)
___ o'clock

7)
___ o'clock

8)
___ o'clock

9)
___ o'clock

Time

Circle the correct time that matches the clock face.

1)
A) 8 o'clock
B) 1 o'clock
C) 2 o'clock
D) 5 o'clock

2)
A) 4 o'clock
B) 7 o'clock
C) 6 o'clock
D) 11 o'clock

3)
A) 9 o'clock
B) 3 o'clock
C) 7 o'clock
D) 5 o'clock

4)
A) 11 o'clock
B) 5 o'clock
C) 4 o'clock
D) 7 o'clock

5)
A) 4 o'clock
B) 10 o'clock
C) 9 o'clock
D) 7 o'clock

6)
A) 2 o'clock
B) 1 o'clock
C) 7 o'clock
D) 8 o'clock

7)
A) 6 o'clock
B) 10 o'clock
C) 1 o'clock
D) 5 o'clock

8)
A) 7 o'clock
B) 6 o'clock
C) 4 o'clock
D) 1 o'clock

9)
A) 6 o'clock
B) 1 o'clock
C) 8 o'clock
D) 11 o'clock

Time

Circle the correct time that matches the clock face.

1) Ⓐ 10 o'clock
    Ⓑ 1 o'clock
    Ⓒ 2 o'clock
    Ⓓ 4 o'clock

2) Ⓐ 6 o'clock
    Ⓑ 2 o'clock
    Ⓒ 4 o'clock
    Ⓓ 8 o'clock

3) Ⓐ 2 o'clock
    Ⓑ 9 o'clock
    Ⓒ 6 o'clock
    Ⓓ 8 o'clock

4) Ⓐ 9 o'clock
    Ⓑ 11 o'clock
    Ⓒ 3 o'clock
    Ⓓ 8 o'clock

5) Ⓐ 4 o'clock
    Ⓑ 5 o'clock
    Ⓒ 3 o'clock
    Ⓓ 1 o'clock

6) Ⓐ 11 o'clock
    Ⓑ 4 o'clock
    Ⓒ 3 o'clock
    Ⓓ 1 o'clock

7) Ⓐ 5 o'clock
    Ⓑ 4 o'clock
    Ⓒ 10 o'clock
    Ⓓ 6 o'clock

8) Ⓐ 6 o'clock
    Ⓑ 2 o'clock
    Ⓒ 8 o'clock
    Ⓓ 9 o'clock

9) Ⓐ 3 o'clock
    Ⓑ 8 o'clock
    Ⓒ 6 o'clock
    Ⓓ 1 o'clock

Time

Look at the clock faces below and enter the correct time.

1)

Half past ____

2)

Half past ____

3)

Half past ____

4)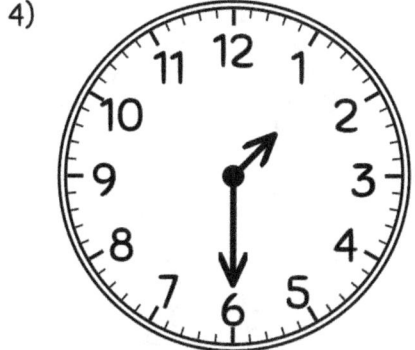

Half past ____

5)

Half past ____

6)

Half past ____

7)

Half past ____

8)

Half past ____

9)

Half past ____

Time

Look at the clock faces below and enter the correct time.

1)
Half past _____

2)
Half past _____

3)
Half past _____

4)
Half past _____

5)
Half past _____

6)
Half past _____

7)
Half past _____

8)
Half past _____

9)
Half past _____

Time

Circle the correct time that matches the clock face.

1) Ⓐ Half past 3:00
    Ⓑ Half past 5:00
    Ⓒ Half past 10:00
    Ⓓ Half past 8:00

2) Ⓐ Half past 9:00
    Ⓑ Half past 8:00
    Ⓒ Half past 3:00
    Ⓓ Half past 7:00

3) Ⓐ Half past 1:00
    Ⓑ Half past 9:00
    Ⓒ Half past 8:00
    Ⓓ Half past 2:00

4) Ⓐ Half past 8:00
    Ⓑ Half past 6:00
    Ⓒ Half past 2:00
    Ⓓ Half past 5:00

5) Ⓐ Half past 7:00
    Ⓑ Half past 10:00
    Ⓒ Half past 8:00
    Ⓓ Half past 1:00

6) Ⓐ Half past 9:00
    Ⓑ Half past 10:00
    Ⓒ Half past 11:00
    Ⓓ Half past 3:00

7) Ⓐ Half past 4:00
    Ⓑ Half past 6:00
    Ⓒ Half past 10:00
    Ⓓ Half past 2:00

8) Ⓐ Half past 5:00
    Ⓑ Half past 8:00
    Ⓒ Half past 6:00
    Ⓓ Half past 7:00

9) Ⓐ Half past 2:00
    Ⓑ Half past 3:00
    Ⓒ Half past 6:00
    Ⓓ Half past 5:00

Time

Circle the correct time that matches the clock face.

1)
A) Half past 11:00
B) Half past 3:00
C) Half past 1:00
D) Half past 7:00

2)
A) Half past 3:00
B) Half past 8:00
C) Half past 11:00
D) Half past 10:00

3)
A) Half past 3:00
B) Half past 10:00
C) Half past 8:00
D) Half past 7:00

4)
A) Half past 3:00
B) Half past 2:00
C) Half past 6:00
D) Half past 8:00

5)
A) Half past 5:00
B) Half past 8:00
C) Half past 7:00
D) Half past 9:00

6)
A) Half past 9:00
B) Half past 6:00
C) Half past 11:00
D) Half past 5:00

7)
A) Half past 4:00
B) Half past 10:00
C) Half past 11:00
D) Half past 5:00

8)
A) Half past 4:00
B) Half past 5:00
C) Half past 1:00
D) Half past 8:00

9)
A) Half past 2:00
B) Half past 11:00
C) Half past 6:00
D) Half past 7:00

FREE WORD SEARCH PACK

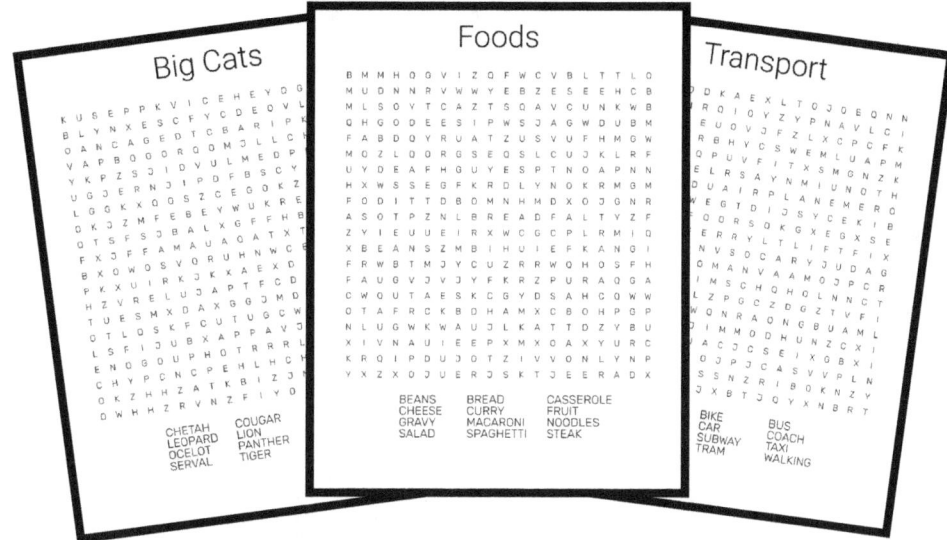

Simply scan the QR code below to get your FREE Word Search pack.

www.ingramcontent.com/pod-product-compliance
Lightning Source LLC
Chambersburg PA
CBHW060426010526

44118CB00017B/2372